Strategies for the Threshold #11

Dealing with Rachab:
Spirit of Wasting

Anne Hamilton

Dealing with Rachab: Spirit of Wasting

Strategies for the Threshold #11

© Anne Hamilton 2025

Published by Armour Books
P. O. Box 492, Corinda QLD 4075 Australia

Cover images: Kevin Carden | 'My Sheep Hear My Voice'; iloveotto 'Asia style textures and backgrounds' | canstockphoto.com; Diego Passadori 'Brown wooden surface' | Unsplash.com

Section divider: microvectorone | Creative Fabrica

Interior Design and Typeset by Beckon Creative

ISBN: 978-1-925380-87-3

A catalogue record for this book is available from the National Library of Australia

All rights reserved. No part of this publication may be reproduced, stored in, or introduced into a retrieval system, or transmitted, in any form, or by any means (electronic, mechanical, photocopying, recording or otherwise) without the prior written permission of the publisher.

Note: Australian spelling and grammar conventions are used throughout this book.

Strategies for the Threshold #11

Dealing with Rachab:
Spirit of Wasting

Anne Hamilton

Scripture quotations marked ASV are taken from the American Standard Version of the Bible. Public domain.

Scripture quotations marked AMP are taken from the Amplified Version of the Bible Copyright © 2015 by The Lockman Foundation, La Habra, CA 90631. All rights reserved. www.lockman.org

Scripture quotations marked BSB are taken from the The Holy Bible, Berean Study Bible, BSB Copyright ©2016 by Bible Hub Used by Permission. All Rights Reserved Worldwide.

Scripture quotations marked ESV are taken from the ESV® Bible (The Holy Bible, English Standard Version®), copyright © 2001 by Crossway, a publishing ministry of Good News Publishers. Used by permission. All rights reserved.

Scripture quotations marked GWT are taken from GOD'S WORD®, a copyrighted work of God's Word to the Nations. Quotations are used by permission. Copyright 1995 by God's Word to the Nations. All rights reserved.

Scripture quotations marked ISV are taken from the Holy Bible: International Standard Version®. Copyright © 1996-forever by The ISV Foundation. ALL RIGHTS RESERVED INTERNATIONALLY. Used by permission.

Scripture quotations marked KJV are taken from the King James Version of the Bible. Public domain.

Scripture quotations marked NASB are taken from the New American Standard Bible®, Copyright © 1960, 1962, 1963, 1968, 1971, 1972, 1973, 1975, 1977, 1995 by The Lockman Foundation. Used by permission. (www.Lockman.org)

Scripture quotations marked NIV are taken from the Holy Bible, New International Version®, NIV®. Copyright © 1973, 1978, 1984, 2011 by Biblica, Inc.™ Used by permission of Zondervan. All rights reserved worldwide. www.zondervan.com The "NIV" and "New International Version" are trademarks registered in the United States Patent and Trademark Office by Biblica, Inc.™.

Scripture quotations marked NKJV are taken from the New King James Version. Copyright © 1982 by Thomas Nelson, Inc. Used by permission. All rights reserved.

Scripture quotations marked NLT are taken from the Holy Bible, New Living Translation, copyright 1996, 2004. Used by permission of Tyndale House Publishers, Inc., Wheaton, Illinois 60189. All rights reserved.

Scripture quotations marked NRS are taken from New Revised Standard Version of the Bible, copyright 1952 [2nd edition, 1971] by the Division of Christian Education of the National Council of the Churches of Christ in the United States of America. Used by permission. All rights reserved.

Scripture quotations marked RSV are taken from the Revised Standard Version of the Bible, copyright © 1946, 1952, and 1971 the Division of Christian Education of the National Council of the Churches of Christ in the United States of America. Used by permission. All rights reserved.

Scripture quotations marked WEB are taken from the World English Bible, a modernisation of the American Standard Version (ASV). Public domain.

Other Books By Anne Hamilton

Jesus and the Healing of History Series

1 ***Like Wildflowers, Suddenly***
2 ***Bent World, Bright Wings***
3 ***Silk Shadows, Rings of Gold***
4 ***Where His Feet Pass***
5 ***The Singing Silence***
6 ***In the Meshes of the Net***
7 ***Interpreted by Love***

Devotional Theology series

God's Poetry: The Identity & Destiny Encoded in Your Name
God's Panoply: The Armour of God & the Kiss of Heaven
God's Pageantry: The Threshold Guardians & the Covenant Defender
God's Pottery: The Sea of Names & the Pierced Inheritance
God's Priority: World-Mending & Generational Testing
More Precious than Pearls (with *Natalie Tensen*)
As Resplendent As Rubies (with *Natalie Tensen*)
As Exceptional as Sapphires (with *Donna Ho*)
Spiritual Legal Rights (with *Janice Sergison*)
Spiritual Legal Rights II (with *Janice Sergison*)

Mystery, Majesty and Mathematics in John's Gospel

The Elijah Tapestry: John 1 and 21
The Summoning of Time: John 2 and 20
The Lustral Waters: John 3 and 19

To:

Gary and Ingrid

Thanks

Jenny
Jenny
Jenny
Jenny
Jess
Joy
Janice
Janne
James
Jill

Contents

Foreword		11
Introduction		13
1	**Awake, Awake!**	17
	Prayer	54
2	**The Do-Nothing**	57
	Prayer	75
3	**Atonement and Covenant**	77
	Prayer	96
4	**Broken Haloes**	99
	Prayer	148
5	**Binding**	151
	Prayer	176
6	**Kinsman-redeemer**	179
	Prayer	209
7	**Against the Cabal**	213
	Prayers	232
Appendix 1 Summary		237
Appendix 2 Glossary of Selected Terms		241
Endnotes		247

Foreword

IF YOU HAVEN'T YET READ the other books in this series, *Strategies for the Threshold*, I strongly recommend you do so. Particularly helpful as background to this book are *Hidden in the Cleft: True and False Refuge* and *Dealing with Azazel: Spirit of Rejection*.

Dealing with Rachab assumes a familiarity with the terminology of the previous books and, while I've summarised key concepts, I haven't spelled them out in detail. Nor have I mentioned all the relevant nuances that are teased out in the earlier parts of this series.

Some terms along with short definitions are listed in the second appendix to refresh your memory. Be aware that this book mainly deals with what happens when all the threshold spirits unite together in common cause to take us down. There are no easy answers to that scenario. No, that's not true: the answer is of course Jesus. But He didn't have any easy answers either.

You are likely to be horrified at how successful these spirits are in shutting down your relationship with Him and who they enlist as their allies in ensuring your calling remains inaccessible. So take your time with the prayers, using them as prompts for the Holy Spirit to guide you just where you need to go to navigate through the wasting in your life.

Much of this book is unapologetically confrontational. Across many decades I've watched too many people walk away from church, and sometimes from God as well, to tread softly or mildly now. This book is about the destruction of faith—the wasting of devotion and the dissolution of belief—through the complicity of authorities with the enemies of our souls. The strategy of our adversaries—the threshold guardians led by the spirit of wasting—is simple. They give up testing us and instead hunt for someone willing to use our loyalty against us. And getting out of that trap requires the very faith that is crumbling around us.

But then there's Jesus...

Grace and peace

Anne

New Year's Day 2025

Introduction

IT HAPPENS ALL THE TIME.

Jenny and her husband went into business. They prayed about it, diligently researched the product they wanted to sell, thoroughly investigated all the rental properties that offered prime exposure for their fledgling enterprise, purchased stock, signed a contract for a lease on a shop, organised an advertising blitz, left their jobs and...

...it all went splat.

Just as they opened, construction work started outside their store and, with access to the entrance so heavily restricted, customers were almost non-existent. They struggled for a few months before being advised to cut their losses and get out while they could.

But finding a new job wasn't easy for either of them. They'd lost their life savings in setting up the business venture and were rapidly sinking into deep debt.

It's such a common story. For every spectacular risk that pays off for an entrepreneur, there are two dozen that fail to reach the ten-year mark.[1] In fact, one in every three start-ups close within two years.

So how do we overcome the spirit of wasting?

That question is answered in *Dealing with Azazel: Spirit of Rejection* and, to be honest, I have very little to add in this book to what I said there.

The issue I particularly want to address now is not so much prevailing over Rachab, since it's so simple—if not especially easy—but the complexity of the warfare we face when the spirit of wasting marshals *all the other* threshold spirits in one hellish cabal to pull us down and take back every toeprint of territory we've gained. God might have promised us that we will inherit wherever we put the soles of our feet, but with seven throne guardians all conspiring together against us to deprive us of the calling we've embarked on as well as tear down every gain we've made, it's all too easy to stumble and find ourselves unable to rise again.

The strategy of the threshold spirits is both diabolic and devastating. They know that, if we've tackled our false refuges and renounced any ungodly covenants God has revealed, and taken steps to show we are seriously committed to Him and demonstrated that our loyalty, though imperfect, is steadfast—as theirs was not—then He will absolutely defend us against their wiles and schemes. So long as we are in covenantal union with Jesus, then nothing can touch us and nothing can stop us from fulfilling the assignments He has attached to the mantle He has given us. So they have to find a way to break that covenantal union and deny us access to the atonement.

When the Israelites were on the threshold of entering the Promised Land, the king of Moab became concerned about their presence on his borders. He therefore employed the diviner Balaam to place a curse on them. Balaam came and gave it his best shot—three times—but he was repeatedly constrained by God to bless the Israelites. Eventually, to earn his pay, Balaam gave the king of Moab a strategy to implement. Since God would not violate His covenant with His people, Balaam advised the king it was necessary to entice the Israelites to breach the covenant themselves. He recommended that a trap be set so that, if the bait were taken, the Israelites would automatically divest themselves of God's covering and divine protection.

Now this tactic, successful as it so often is, is not the one that the threshold guardians use against us. Instead their signature scheme is a malign variation on Balaam's ploy. Yet the net result is the same—we lose the covenantal defence of God. We are set up in such a way that retaliation is unavoidable, rejection is inevitable, every choice is a strangling snare and wasting is staring us in the face with a vicious smirk.

Whereas in the past, we might have been complicit with Python, Ziz, Leviathan, Azazel, Belial or Lilith, that's no longer the case. In fact, these threshold spirits have now turned their attention from us and are focused instead on finding someone with the authority to restrain us, preferably permanently.

Balaam was an enemy in the pay of another enemy. The threshold guardians are no longer seeking an enemy like Balaam to do us harm, but a leader and preferably a friend with the right to speak into our lives—someone who can be convinced that we need to be brought back under control but who can also be influenced to cross the line into deception and betrayal when we choose obedience to God over obedience to them.

Negotiating this kind of minefield is entirely different.

1

Awake, Awake!

Done is a battle on the dragon black,
Our champion Christ conquered his force,
The gates of hell are broken with a crack,
The sign triumphant is the Cross.

William Dunbar
Done is a battell on the dragon blak

THE SPIRIT OF RAHAB is not the same as the woman Rahab. One is a chaos monster, a fearsome denizen of the deep, and the other is a resident of Jericho who saved a pair of spies. You'll find them spelled exactly the same way in English translations of Scripture but I've made a difference to hopefully avoid confusion.[2]

There are six references to Rachab the sea monster in Scripture and three of them refer to some primordial battle when the Lord overcame it:

> *Awake, awake, put on strength, arm of Yahweh! Awake, as in the days of old, the generations of ancient times. Isn't it You who cut Rahab in pieces, who pierced the monster?*
>
> Isaiah 51:9 WEB

> *With His power He quieted the sea, and by His understanding He shattered Rahab.*
>
> Job 26:12 NASB

> *You crushed Rahab like a carcass; You scattered Your enemies with Your mighty arm.*
>
> Psalm 89:10 BSB

Another two references symbolise Egypt as Rachab 'the Do-Nothing'.[3]

> *Egypt's help is worthless and empty; therefore I have called her 'Rahab who sits still.'*
>
> Isaiah 30:7 ESV

> *Among those who know Me I mention Rahab and Babylon; behold, Philistia and Tyre, with Cush—'This one was born there,' they say.*
>
> Psalm 87:4 ESV

The last reference is ambiguous: it may refer to Egypt or it may refer to spiritual courtiers who attend Rachab:

> *God does not hold back His anger. Even Rahab's helpers bow humbly in front of Him.*
>
> Job 9:13 GWT

Now all of this is very comforting imagery for us. God is the valiant warrior who, long ago, smote Rachab the dragon who lived in the sea and can therefore easily dispose of the spiritual power of the same ilk. The ancient Israelites might have looked to Egypt as a false refuge and helper in times of trouble, but it's to be hoped that we don't look to Rachab in the same way.

The name Rachab has the sense of *being wide or broad, to expand or grow large, to spread out* or *be spacious, to have* or *make room*. Now the spirit of wasting can operate for long periods at quite low levels in our lives —exercising slow but deep attrition that ensures we never get ahead. As soon as the prospect of getting out of debt, for example, dawns on the horizon, we're hit with an unexpected financial outlay that takes us back to square one. However Rachab ramps up its activity when we approach the threshold into our calling—that's when we find ourselves plunged into calamity and experiencing devastating losses. All that we've worked to achieve is swept away. A perfect storm of circumstances seems to conspire against us, just as we're ready to take up the mantle we sense God is holding out for us.

And 'perfect storm' is the right description since the meaning of Rahab, as opposed to Rachab, is *storm, proud, defiant, arrogant, boisterous*.

The closest ally of the spirit of wasting is Python, the spirit of constriction. Often what happens is that, when we've resisted Python and it releases its hold on us, we have an intoxicating sense of freedom as the pressure disappears. We move out into a broad, expansive place and we drop our guard. We sense that Python has been overcome, we thank God and we get on with the task He's set us. But, if we're not wise and cautious, soon we find ourselves spread so thin—perhaps financially, perhaps emotionally, perhaps relationally, perhaps time-wise—that we're heading for burnout. Suddenly there are so many demands on us from so many different directions we don't even know how to begin to prioritise them, let alone fulfil them.

Burnout can take years to recover from—years wasted because we fell for one of the enemy's deadly schemes. Still, never forget that the Lord Jesus is the redeemer of wasted time.

There are other ways Rachab can make inroads into our lives. One symptom of the presence of wasting is the feeling of being stuck, as if we're running in place, expending a lot of energy but getting nowhere. Now it's important to distinguish this kind of stuckness from what happens with Lilith. When wasting is at work in our lives, we feel like we're on a treadmill. However, when the vampire spirit is in operation, we sense that we're staked by trauma to a particular moment in time. Both spirits are working to exhaust us, but in different ways—Lilith by draining our resurrection life, Rachab by pushing us to exert just a little more effort until we collapse under overload.

Another symptom is procrastination.[4] If it's a besetting problem, then we're likely to be complicit with wasting. And if we're apt to stall, delay, postpone and defer any action on a troubling issue in the hope that, if we put off doing anything for long enough, the difficulties will either resolve themselves or else go away, then we've definitely got an agreement with wasting. Rachab is a chaos-bringer—and it's no coincidence that, when our inaction or dithering finally reaches crisis point, chaos is the result. We've accepted the invitation to the 'do-nothing' party.

Python pressures us to make a choice—preferably the wrong one. Rachab allures us into wishing that the situation will just go away so we don't have to make a choice. Of course, if the situation doesn't vanish, then not making a choice is never a neutral position but is preferring one side or the other by default.

Clearly, all the usual procedures apply when it comes to procrastination:

- Repent of using it as a false refuge.
- Renounce any covenants with the spirit of wasting.
- Take responsibility for the choice you select.

Even if you've already done this, you may not necessarily be ready to remove Rachab from your life. Before it's possible to overcome wasting, it's necessary to overcome the spirit of rejection. As I pointed out in *Dealing with Azazel*, there are extremely good reasons for this.

Only when you can look the spirit of rejection in the eye and not fight, flee, freeze, flatter, forestall or forget are you ready to face—not Rachab, surprisingly—but the angel named War. This is the commander God deploys on our behalf to drive out all of our enemies, including wasting, in front of us. He asks us to do only one thing to ensure the war goes successfully. Obey.

The Greek equivalent of the spirit of rejection, the scapegoat Azazel, is Pan. A demigod, half-human and half-goat, Pan is credited with engendering the sickening, often irrational, fear named after him: *panic*. Azazel is terrifying.

And as outlined in *Dealing with Azazel*, we are not called to cast it out—because it will always come back since its legal rights cannot be removed—but to *overcome* it. Any attempt to override those rights is counterproductive, since rejection is integral to the Cornerstone of our lives when we are in covenant with Jesus. He, after all, is the Stone who was rejected that nonetheless became the Head of the Corner. If we totally eject rejection from our lives, we're actually asking Jesus to leave. So we have to face the terror and, having done that and stood our ground, we are ready to face God's Terror, the angel He also calls both War and His hornet.

*Behold, I am going to send an angel before you to guard you along the way and to bring you into the place which I have prepared. Be attentive to him and obey his voice; do not be rebellious toward him, for he will not pardon your rebellion, since My name is **IN HIM**. But if you truly obey his voice and do all that I say, then I will be an enemy to your enemies and an adversary to your adversaries... and I will completely destroy them.*

You shall not worship their gods, nor serve them, nor do according to their deeds; but you shall utterly overthrow them and break their memorial stones in pieces. And you shall serve the Lord your God, and He will bless your bread and your water; and I will remove sickness from your midst. There will be no one miscarrying or unable to have children in your land; I will fulfill the number of your days.

I will send My terror ahead of you, and throw into confusion all the people among whom you come... And I will send hornets ahead of you... I will not drive them out from you in a single year, so that the land will not become desolate and the animals of the field become too numerous for you. I will drive them out from you little by little, until you become fruitful and take possession of the land...

I will give into your hands the people who live in the land, and you will drive them out before you. Do not make a covenant with them or with their gods. Do not let them live in your land or they will cause you to sin against Me, because the worship of their gods will certainly be a snare to you.

Exodus 23:20–33 NASB

Now it may not be obvious from this passage that the name of the angel is War. However the Hebrew word for the phrase emphasised above in bold, IN HIM, is also the word for *war*.

'My name is War,' says God. We're apt to think of Yahweh Shalom, *the Lord is peace*, as an appropriate name but sometimes forget He is also Yahweh Sabaoth, *the Lord of Hosts, the God of Angel Armies*, as well as Ish Milchamah, *a Man of War*.

Although the Hebrew words for *war* are different in the following verses, both have double meanings:

> *'My name is in him* [War]*.'*

Exodus 23:21 NASB

and

> *'The Lord is a man of war* [bread]*: the Lord is His name.'*

Exodus 15:3 KJV

The description of the angel called Terror, Hornet and War occurs when God is making promises to the Israelites during a covenant ceremony at Mount Sinai. He is pledging that His angel will go ahead of the people and drive out their enemies. He cautions the people not to defy the angel. Implicit in this direction is that the angel has just one purpose: War. If the people do not follow his commands, then he will war against them.

The angel has a strategic battleplan to take and hold ground; he's not going to conduct a lightning strike whereby the entire land will be conquered in a single year. It will be a slow process so that all gains can be maintained and no wasting occurs. No void will be created that can be filled by an influx of wild animals. God further promises that, once the people occupy the inheritance He is granting them, He will bless them if they continue to obey. Food and water will be abundant, sickness will be absent, people will live the full span of their days. In other words, no wasting will occur. God has commissioned His angel to drive out poverty, lack and disease.

Now, as it happened, it was forty years before the angel named War could move on his assignment. The delay was the result of a report by ten of the twelve spies sent to scout out the land. The giants had so intimidated them they said it couldn't be conquered. Apparently, they either didn't believe the Terror was up to the job, or else they forgot God's promise it would drive out their enemies before them.

However, once they were committed to the task of taking up their inheritance four decades later, the Terror made its presence known. Instead of twelve spies, Joshua the leader of all the tribes of Israel and the commander of their army, sent out just two. They made their way into Jericho and sought lodging with an inn-keeper and prostitute named, of course, Rahab. How better for God to tell us that the spirit of wasting is no match for God's agent, Terror, than to have a woman with such a name speak of the dread that has fallen upon the land? This was forty years after the crossing of the Red Sea but the inhabitants of Jericho were still scared stiff at its implications. They knew God wasn't on their side. Rahab told the two spies:

> *I know that the Lord has given you the land, and that dread of you has fallen on us, and that all the inhabitants of the land melt in fear before you.*

Joshua 2:9 NRS

The importance of being able to look the Terror in the eye and then subject ourselves in obedience is demonstrated by Joshua's encounter with the commander of the Lord's hosts.

> *Now when Joshua was by Jericho, he looked up, and behold, a man was standing opposite him with his drawn sword in his hand, and Joshua went to him and said to him, 'Are you for us or for our adversaries?'*

> *He said, 'No; rather I have come now as captain of the army of the Lord.'*
>
> *Then Joshua fell with his face toward the earth and bowed down, and said to him, 'What does my lord have to say to his servant?'*
>
> *The captain of the Lord's army said to Joshua, 'Remove your sandals from your feet, because the place where you are standing is holy...'*
>
> Joshua 5:13–15 AMP

Any assumption that God is always *'for us'* should mean that we are taken aback by these words of the angel. His answer as to which side he's on is a simple NO. The question is completely wrong. The angel called War doesn't align himself with us, we have to choose to ally ourselves with God through obedience to His angelic battle commander. Like Joshua, we simply have to be able to ask, 'What are God's orders?' And then we have to follow through on them. Even if they are as mysterious as: walk round this town in silence for six days, and on the seventh day, walk around it seven times. Then shout!

Our ability to lay hold of the promises of God to us depends not only on our willingness to obey Him but on our ability to face the Terror. To do that, we have to have mastered the spirit of rejection in our lives. That means we're not going to panic when rejection comes calling; we're not going to rush to hide in a false refuge; we're instead going to seek God and ask His will for the moment.

At the end of the day, the strategy for overcoming Rachab is beyond simple. It's this:

- Overcome rejection
- Allow God to deploy His angel, War, on our behalf.
- Obey the angel, lest he war against us.
- Remember that his work of conquest will be slow so that we can maintain what he achieves.
- Occupy the ground he wins on our behalf.

The hardest part is the overcoming of rejection. Obeying and occupying are not so easy, either. At the beginning of the Book of Judges, the angel leaves.

> *The angel of the Lord went up from Gilgal to Bokim and said, 'I brought you up out of Egypt and led you into the land I swore to give to your ancestors. I said, "I will never break My covenant with you, and you shall not make a covenant with the people of this land, but you shall break down their altars." Yet you have disobeyed Me. Why have you done this? And I have also said, "I will not drive them out before you; they will become traps for you, and their gods will become snares to you."'*
>
> *When the angel of the Lord had spoken these things to all the Israelites, the people wept aloud.*
>
> Judges 2:1–4 NIV

It's clear that the Terror can not only turn against us if we disobey, but can leave us. God's strategy for overturning wasting in our lives can therefore be undone by our own refusal to comply with His directions. We see this principle in operation much more clearly in the life of Elijah than elsewhere.

After Elijah's monumental triumph at Mount Carmel against the prophets of Baal-Hadad and Asherah, the spirit of wasting snatches back victory out of the jaws of defeat by terrorising him through Jezebel. It becomes clear from his conversation with God that, in fact, he'd never overcome the spirit of rejection, the necessary precursor to removing wasting. When faced with a death threat, he panicked and fled.

Our inability to face rejection has profound consequences. It's not just rejection that we can't overcome, it's also wasting. I've looked at Elijah several times in different books[5] in the light of Jesus' recapitulation of his storyline so that God's intended outcome prevails.

Recapitulation is a theological term used in early church history. It's the earliest theory of the atonement, and it describes how Jesus reversed the sin of Adam. Where Adam had been tempted in a garden and fell, bringing death into the world, Jesus resisted the temptation and instead brought life for mankind. Where once death came from a choice involving believing God about a tree, now life comes from a choice involving believing in Jesus about the tree of the Cross. Jesus, in reworking the storyline, mended the primal wound of the world.

Now I've extended the concept of recapitulation beyond the death and resurrection of Jesus into His every action. In my view, it's simply a technical term for healing history. Every story about Him resounds with echoes of the past[6] but it's easy to miss them because, at a critical juncture, He changed the plotline of the story. And by examining the consequences of His alteration, we can discover what was meant to be.

So, when it comes to Elijah, it's possible to uncover his singular failure because of what Jesus did to fix it. Elijah's mission was to change the government of Samaria and bring the people back to God. He'd removed the court councillors, the four hundred and fifty prophets of Baal. But, because of his repeated dereliction of duty in following up on God's directions, another four hundred of them are back within a few years, advising the king once again. Elijah never takes the opportunity that comes his way to complete the assignment God gave him at Mount Horeb—to anoint Jehu king of Israel. Neither does he make the opportunity to anoint Hazael king of Aram.

Now many writers simply cannot believe Elijah didn't fulfil this commission. They presume he was obedient to the Lord's command. It is inconceivable, in their view, to think Elijah would have defied God and, therefore, the silence of Scripture indicates he carried out his charge. After all, as some commentators point out, while Scripture doesn't say Elijah performed the anointings, it doesn't say he didn't either—therefore, we can assume he did.

Personally I don't think the silence of Scripture can be interpreted to suggest something is more likely to have happened than not. Particularly when we can spot a recapitulation, a modification of the story, in the life of Jesus. There are only two breakfasts of bread baked on hot coals in Scripture. Both occur when a man called by God was running away from his vocation. The first happened near Beersheba when Elijah woke to find an angelic meal that fortified him to flee forty days south to the mountain of God. The second happened on the shores of the Lake of Galilee when Jesus restored Simon Peter after his triple denial.[7]

The second story tells us how the first was meant to play out. Elijah was given the food of angels not to go on, but to turn back. So let's look at the might-have-been had he chosen to do so. At that moment in time, his chance to change the government of Samaria was on the cusp of being lost. The power vacuum he'd created by executing the prophets of Baal was time-sensitive and would soon be filled. If he returned, he could ask Obadiah, the king's steward who'd protected a hundred prophets, to usher them out of the caves where they were hidden. Elijah could use his new-won authority to have them appointed king's councillors. But he didn't go back.

Down at Horeb, God gave him another way of changing the government—through anointing Jehu. But, despite meeting up with Jehu at one time and despite the fact that Jehu was stationed at a fortress outpost just a few kilometres from Elijah's own hometown,[8] he let the chances slip on by.

Eventually, Peter was commissioned by Jesus to complete the assignment that had been waiting more than eight centuries for fulfillment: the ingathering of the Gentiles. That's what the anointing of Hazael was supposed to achieve—as we can see by comparing Hazael with the first Gentile convert, Cornelius.[9] However neither Elijah, nor Elisha after him, was prepared to offer a knowledge of Yahweh to anyone born outside the bounds of Israel. They also deferred the anointing of Jehu for decades.

What we see in the story of Elijah is an example of massive wasting as a result of panic. Jezebel had issued a death threat by invoking the gods. If she didn't kill him, they were free to kill her. In other words, she'd invited them to be part of the vengeance she was about to exact. And who were these gods? They were the so-called young lions, the sons of Asherah and the brothers of Baal-Hadad. Both Asherah and Baal-Hadad had just been defeated by Yahweh through the agency of Elijah. Baal-Hadad, the storm-god and king of the Canaanite pantheon, had been shown up as a powerless weakling, and his prophets killed. It's unclear what happened to the prophets of Asherah. And that may be significant because, as we shall see, another name for Rachab is Asherah.[10]

Now Elijah was clearly terrified of the threat of the 69 brothers of Baal. Their sister, Anat, the war goddess who revelled in frenzied carnage and who liked to wade in blood and fasten her enemies' heads to her belt, would have been summoned to lead the charge.[11] This was not a baseless fear on Elijah's part. Basically Jezebel had mobilised the principalities of the nations, all of them in one go, to attack him.

So who is the angel who cooks a breakfast that can sustain a person for forty days? Surely, given the circumstances, it's the Terror. The one who, if we obey him, will war on our behalf and drive out wasting.

Yet wasting is precisely what happens to Elijah. He does not bring about regime change—though it would have been so easy at that moment. He's got the people onside and he's got the backing of the king's steward who, in turn, is supported by one hundred prophets. Despite his three-times reiterated statement that he is the only prophet left, it's not true. He seems to have forgotten what Obadiah told him. We are introduced to several of those prophets in succeeding chapters as they variously advise or challenge the king.

Perhaps the most tragic aspect of all this wasting is Elijah's loss of calling.

Just before he dies in battle, Ahab makes a scandalous admission to the king of Judah. He says there's only one prophet of Yahweh left and he hates him. Although Elijah and Elisha are still alive, Ahab doesn't name them. He names Micaiah. Either Ahab no longer considers that Elijah represents Yahweh or he no longer considers him to be a prophet.

This is precisely the goal of the spirit of wasting—to rob us of our calling, right at the moment when we should be celebrating the defeat of our enemies.

Jesus once told this parable:

> *Whenever an unclean spirit goes out of a person, it wanders through dry places looking for a place to rest but doesn't find any. So it says, 'I will go back to my home that I left.' When it gets back home, it finds it swept clean and put in order. Then it goes and brings with it seven other spirits more evil than itself, and they all go in and settle there. And so the final condition of that person is worse than the first.*
>
> Luke 11:24–26 ISV

When we've overcome the spirit of rejection, when the Terror has driven out the spirit of wasting, when we've worked in partnership with Jesus to defeat Leviathan, Ziz, Python, Belial and Lilith, they're not done with us. Like the unclean spirit that returns to find its former dwelling place to be clean and orderly and therefore gathers a group of friends to prowl around until they discover a way back in, so all these threshold guardians unite in looking for a back door. Now we might have been diligent in our spiritual cleansing and dead-locked that door, triple-bolted it and double-barred it. But the spirits know we'll open up to someone we trust or, alternatively, someone in authority over us. We may even have given keys to the back door to that 'trustworthy' individual. So that's who the threshold guardians go searching for: the person with the power in our lives to grant them access back in.

Elijah didn't trust Jezebel. Far from it. Yet he allowed her to have authority over him. He ceded power to her by believing that God could not protect him from her death threat. When we believe the lies of others and act on them, we give them significant power over us.

Elijah is the first person recorded in Scripture as raising someone from the dead. He bursts onto the scene without introduction when he fronts up to Ahab, the king of Samaria, and informs him that not a drop of rain is going to fall again until he—Elijah—gives the word. And then he disappears.

He's not seen again for more than three years. At that time, he engineers a climactic confrontation on Mount Carmel with the spiritual advisors of Ahab's government—hundreds of prophets who are responsible for ensuring the fertility of the land by their sacrifices to Baal and Asherah. Now it may seem like the war with these deities began when Elijah called for the showdown on the mountain, but it actually started when he declared the drought. What he effectively said at that moment was: 'Baal-Hadad, your storm-god, the king of the young lions who are the sons of the goddess Asherah, is a fraud. He doesn't control the weather. Yahweh does, and I am His appointed mouthpiece.'

No doubt the prophets of Baal-Hadad simply laughed this off, called on the 'Cloud-rider' to appear and bring rain in its season, and waited... waited... waited... as the parched land withered beneath the unrelenting sun. Meantime, Elijah spent some time at the brook Cherith where he was fed by ravens. When the stream dried up, Elijah followed God's direction to leave Israel. Ahab then became desperate, even demanding reassurances from neighbouring kings that they were not harbouring the one and only person who could end the famine in Samaria.

God had, in fact, sent Elijah to Zarephath—the very place Ahab was least likely to look. And, even if he did check it out and he happened to discover Elijah's hiding place, Ahab wasn't going to threaten the ruler of that territory or go to war with him. That was because Zarephath was in the region of Tyre and Sidon, and the king there was Ahab's wife's father, the priest Ethbaal.

God had planted Elijah right in the heart of enemy territory—and told him to rely on an impoverished widow for provision. Back in Samaria, the prophets of Baal and Asherah were wining and fine dining at Jezebel's table, while Elijah was experiencing common and, very probably, non-kosher fare in a foreign country.

If Elijah learned nothing else, he should have realised that God was not only protecting him and providing for him, but He was also protecting the widow, her son *and* the people of the nations around Samaria from a trumped-up excuse for a war. Did it ever dawn on him that God loved the people of Zarephath and wanted them to know about Him?

Sometime in the year or two that Elijah was in Zarephath, the widow's son died. And Elijah was instrumental in raising him from the dead. This is the first instance of this type of miraculous intervention from God on record. Elijah was collaborating with God in unprecedented ways—ways that seemed to defy the natural order:

- commanding the rain to stop
- receiving daily food drops of bread and meat from birds notorious for not feeding their young

- providing for the widow and her son through a jar of flour and a cruse of oil that would not run dry until rain fell on the land
- raising a young man from the dead.

The care and protection of God was abundant and evident.

Finally Elijah returned to Samaria. The first person who recognised him was the king's steward, Obadiah, who was out looking for fodder. Now their interaction is exceptionally important if we want to progress towards understanding Elijah's downfall. Obadiah revealed he'd been sheltering a hundred prophets of Yahweh from the murderous wrath of Ahab and Jezebel. These prophets were holed up in two caves and were being regularly provided bread and water. Three of them actually turn up later in the narrative, one acting as an itinerant war counsellor for Ahab during the conflict with Ben-hadad[12] of Aram. Obadiah, it becomes clear, was not only loyal to Yahweh but had risked his life for those who shared his faith.

Now Elijah persuaded Obadiah to bring Ahab to him and, when that happened, he proposed the contest on Mount Carmel with the prophets of Baal and Asherah. It was a challenge to determine, once and for all, who was the true God. The people of Samaria were summoned as witnesses and Elijah set out the terms: a sacrificial offering was to be placed on an altar, the name of a deity was to be invoked, and the one who answered in fire from heaven was to be worshipped as the true Lord.

It's here, as Elijah addressed the people, we see the first hint of something wrong.

> *I alone am left a prophet of the Lord; but Baal's prophets are four hundred and fifty men.*
>
> 1 Kings 18:22 NASB

'I alone am left': it's a statement Elijah will repeat twice more when he arrives at Mount Horeb. But it's not true. Even before God revealed that He had reserved to Himself seven thousand faithful people who had not bent the knee to Baal, Elijah should have been aware it wasn't accurate. Obadiah had spoken of a hundred prophets of Yahweh concealed in two caves. Perhaps Elijah was accusing Obadiah of lying. Or perhaps he was trying to help Obadiah by allaying publicly any suspicions Ahab might have had—but I'm inclined to doubt this because he makes the same statement when he's alone with God. Whatever Elijah's reasons for declaring this in the first place, he obviously became utterly convinced of it. Neither his prophetic discernment nor the testimony of Obadiah changed his belief.

Elijah didn't put himself into the hands of the spirit of wasting straight off. First, he allowed himself to be swayed by the spirit of rejection, the one who whispers: *'I alone am left.'* The spirit of rejection is a master at inducing panic. And once Elijah had been tempted into terrified flight, wasting was easy.

Abraham, Noah, Joseph, David, Elisha, Elijah.

It would be hard to put together a line-up of greater heroes of the faith. We tend to look up to these prophets and patriarchs with unstinting and unreserved admiration. They faced intense trials, monumental testing, fierce opposition and enormous obstacles and, even in their humanity, they generally won out. So when we are confronted with difficulties and burdens, usually of much less severity, we can be reassured—knowing that God is no less for us than He was for them.

Yet, each of them made a dishonorable choice at a critical moment and their decisions impacted generation after generation across a rollcall of centuries. Most of these men of faith made more than one such ignoble choice.

I was reading an inspirational article recently about Elijah. It unpacked with deep sensitivity the depression, anguish, breaking and vulnerability he experienced after his greatest triumph. It detailed how, on receiving that death threat from Jezebel, he was so overwhelmed with fear he panicked and ran for his life. Exhausted, defeated and tormented, he just wanted to die—but he journeyed to Mount Horeb and hid in a cave.

The author encouraged any readers facing similar despondency and mental anguish to realise that *'what Elijah did next shifted everything.'*

> *He pulled his cloak over his face and went out and stood at the mouth of the cave.*
>
> 1 Kings 19:13 NIV

And thereafter, as the article went on, Elijah's life changed when he wrapped his mantle around him, listened to God's voice and moved out into his new season. As I've pointed out, this is not a realistic view.

A mantle is a symbol of calling, vocation, destiny, identity. Elisha wanted Elijah's mantle in order to inherit a double portion of his spirit and thereby double his mentor's miracles. But that's not what a mantle is for: it's to finish the incomplete works of those who wore the mantle before us.

Anat wants to dispossess us of any mantle we carry; while Asherah—or Rachab, whatever you'd prefer to call the spirit of wasting—wants to push back on all the gains we've made towards the pursuit of our calling. It doesn't matter which one of them takes us down, the effect is the same, whether our inheritance is stolen or is frittered away.

It's incredibly challenging to find someone with an accurate view of Elijah or, for that matter, an authentic perspective on the other heroes of the faith I've mentioned. We're blinded by haloes so dazzling we don't even notice outright rebellion when it's staring straight at us. Worse than not noticing it, we flip it around, re-interpreting it so that it's a reason for applause and an example to emulate.

Far from a situation where *'what Elijah did next shifted everything'*, what he did shifted *nothing*. The 'new season' of Elijah wasn't about fresh assignments and increasing ardour for God. The 'new season' involved decades of defiance. Elijah wasted the last years of his life by ignoring God's specific instructions:

> *Go back by the way you came, and go to the Desert of Damascus. When you arrive, you are to anoint Hazael as king over Aram. You are also to anoint Jehu... as king over Israel and Elisha... to succeed you as prophet.*
>
> 1 Kings 19:15-16 BSB

Elijah did not carry out the first two directions. He even met up with Jehu once but ignored the opportunity that presented itself.

As I previously mentioned, many commentators simply cannot believe Elijah would have not carried out the tasks God assigned to him. They assume that three unrecorded events similar to the anointing of David took place, long before those chosen by God were actually elevated to high office. The silence of Scripture is read as affirming Elijah's obedience rather than as showing us his recalcitrance.

Yet Ahab pronounces a damning indictment on Elijah, Elisha and the school of prophets following them. It's all too easy to miss its significance. During a state visit by the king of Judah, Jehoshaphat, Ahab tries to manipulate an agreement between them to go to war together against Aram. Jehoshaphat, trapped by several covenants, tries to wangle his way out of it by asking to hear from someone other than the four hundred new prophets of Baal.

> *Jehoshaphat asked, 'Is there no longer a prophet of the Lord here whom we can inquire of?'*
>
> *The king of Israel answered Jehoshaphat, 'There is still one prophet through whom we can inquire of the Lord, but I hate him because he never prophesies anything good about me, but always bad. He is Micaiah son of Imlah.'*
>
> 1 Kings 22:7–8 NIV

Elijah and Elisha are both alive when Ahab gives this answer to Jehoshaphat. There's only one prophet left, he says, echoing Elijah's thrice-repeated declaration, before naming a prophet we didn't even know existed to this point. God had given Elijah a mandate to change the government of Samaria at least a decade previously[13] but, as time went by, it had become evident he was never going to enact it.

Elijah role-modelled insubordination for his successor Elisha who, in turn, handed it on as a pattern for Jonah. It's only when we see that same pattern in the hands of Jesus that we can glimpse what Elijah's unfinished calling really entailed and how breathtakingly serious his downfall was. Think of all the wars that might have been prevented if Aram and Assyria had come to know Yahweh. By the time of Elisha, the Arameans were seeking Yahweh—both Naaman and Hazael come to Elisha but he gives them not a word of teaching to increase their knowledge of Yahweh. As for Jonah, he doesn't follow up on the repentance of the people of Nineveh by telling them about the merciful and compassionate Lord of heaven and earth. They responded merely on a doomsday prophecy, *'Yet forty days and Nineveh shall be overthrown.'*[14] Not a whisper of a word about Yahweh.

Elijah did not end well. His fear of the violent beserker-goddess, Anat, overcame him. It wasn't depression that instigated his panicked flight; rather terror triggered his need to escape and, after running non-stop for six days, exhaustion and fear were the catalysts for depression. Elijah simply didn't trust God to protect him. Jezebel had invoked 'the gods' against him. In running from Anat, the dispossessor, he launched himself straight into the hands of the spirit of wasting. He'd triumphed against Asherah, only to let her seize his victory from him.

His actions shed light on our own behaviour when we allow our victory in Christ to be snatched from our grasp.

A self-destructive, self-sabotaging variety of wasting results from an inability to repent for wrongdoing. There's an example of this in Jephthah's story.

It was the time of the Judges. The people of Israel were under attack by the Ammonites and, in desperation, they called on the outlaw Jephthah to save them. He was the son of a prostitute who'd been banished by his brothers. Having banded together with other outcasts in the land of Tob, Jephthah had become a tough fighter and a shrewd negotiator.

He began his campaign against the Ammonites by attempting diplomacy with their king. When it failed, he stormed through the region devastating twenty Ammonite cities as well as regaining territory that had been lost. Prior to setting out, he'd issued a call to war throughout all Israel. However, the men of Ephraim ignored the call. Perhaps they thought, 'Go to war under the leadership of a harlot's son? No way.'

Whatever their reasoning, after Jephthah returned from the war—spectacularly victorious over the enemy—the men of Ephraim obviously got a little nervous. Jephthah had suddenly emerged as a force to be reckoned with. It was more than possible, at least in the minds of the elders of Ephraim, that he might be annoyed with them for their lack of support.

Why wouldn't he? Tit-for-tat, after all. In the not-so-distant past, the clans of Ephraim were part of a tribal collaboration that had wiped out an entire town for not answering a call to war. That town was Jabesh in Gilead, the very same area Jephthah came from.[15] In fact, the most likely spot for the warriors of Ephraim to have forded the Jordan was just below Jabesh Gilead so, as they saw its ruins on the heights above, that particular bit of recent history might just have floated to the forefront of their minds. Considering Jephthah wasn't likely to forget what had happened at Jabesh Gilead, it would be entirely logical in the view of the Ephraimites for him to take vengeance on two counts: one for the past, one for the present. Given what happened next, this line of thinking was evidently the one followed by the men of Ephraim.

They adopted what Jim Wilder and Ray Woolridge call 'enemy mode'[16]—and, of the three types they've identified, the men of Ephraim chose the most dangerous for both themselves and for others: intelligent enemy mode.

Now, their best approach would have been an apology. But their status amongst the tribes had already been compromised by ignoring a call to war, and an apology would lower their prestige further. So, compounding their unreliability and lack of integrity with grandiose hypocrisy, they instead tried a spot of gas-lighting and intimidation. Having gathered tens of thousands of troops and crossed the Jordan, they marched to Jephthah's place and basically said, 'Why didn't you send for us when you knew you were going to war? We're offended, so we're going to burn your house down with you in it.'

Nothing like an announcement of pre-emptive retaliation to set the right tone for peaceful reconciliation, is there? Not surprisingly, Jephthah happened to be in no mood for games. His daughter was out somewhere on the hills of Gilead, in a period of mourning, because Jephthah had made a rash vow that, if God gave him victory, he'd sacrifice the first thing out of his door when he returned home. He was probably bleak, surly and grumpy.

Now Jephthah might have been diplomatic with the Ammonites but the lies of the men of Ephraim were too much for him. They hadn't sent out a softly-spoken ambassadorial party with an explanation or a request for forgiveness, they'd sent out an attack force spoiling for a fight. They clearly wanted to get Jephthah before he got them. The cohesiveness of their identity as a tribal unit was a tragic part of what happened next.

Now Jephthah probably wasn't prepared for this surprise but he summoned his troops and defended himself with an immediate counterattack. The Ephraimites fled all the way back to the fords of the Jordan. There a band of Jephthah's men confronted the survivors, using a simple test to identify the raiders. 'Say, "Shibboleth",' they'd ask.

42,000 were killed because they said 'Sibboleth' instead. They lost their lives because of their accent.

Or did they?

As Chaim Bentorah points out, it's very unlikely these survivors came up to the fords of the Jordan one by one. There were tens of thousands of them, after all. Most likely, they came up in groups and, once the password 'Shibboleth' was known, it should have very quickly passed back down the line that it would be a good idea to practise the 'sh' sound. But it seems that some of them—perhaps even lots of them—persisted in saying a word that was full of fatal risk.

So did the Ephraimites die because of their accent or because of arrogance? Once the brain gets into enemy mode, particularly the kind described as intelligent enemy mode, there is no option but to win. The person would rather die than lose—whether that's status or some aspect of identity. And both status and identity are involved in saying 'sibboleth' rather than 'shibboleth'.

Because, you see, although both 'shibboleth' and 'sibboleth' mean the same, they have different roots and thus significantly different overtones: one carries humility and the other pride.

As we examine this story closely, we see more than pride, we also see hypocrisy, dishonour, gas-lighting, lying, deception, victim-blaming, injustice, intimidation and death threats, terrorisation, attempted domination and manipulation, taking offence in advance to forestall any objection by the victim about being mistreated, a pre-emptive strike to prevent retaliation for wrongdoing by attacking first—all of this as well as a tactical, pro-active rejection of a new leader.

The incoming Ephraimites reacted to what they imagined Jephthah would do, not what he actually did. They were not confronting a person but their own fears. When we confront our own fears, we have to align with God, not with Python, Ziz, Leviathan, Azazel, Belial, Lilith or Rachab. The men of Ephraim were in such complete complicity with *all* of these threshold spirits, they apparently could not choose to pursue reconciliation. More than simply refusing to repent, they didn't even give Jephthah a chance to forgive them. Instead they announced they were going to burn the house down with him in it. And who knows how many innocent others.

Now Chaim Bentorah indicates there's a lot more going on with 'shibboleth' and 'sibboleth' than just pronunciation. Both mean *an ear of grain*. However, 'shibboleth' comes from 'shobel' which, besides meaning *an ear of grain*, also means *a stream, the skirt of a flowing garment* or *the train of a robe*. On the other hand, 'sibboleth' comes from 'sabal', *to bear a heavy load*.

'Say, "Shibboleth,"' said the men of Gilead, subtly asking for their tribal brothers to speak out an attachment to the hem of a garment. In neighbouring lands, touching the hem of a king's robe was symbolic of loyalty to that sovereign. It was therefore an act of covenantal submission.

We're likely to remember the famous incident where the woman with the issue of blood touched the hem of Jesus' garment, but in fact she was just one among many.

> *People brought all their sick to Him and begged Him to let the sick just touch the edge of His cloak, and all who touched it were healed.*
>
> Matthew 14:35–36 NIV

The people in Jesus' day were doing something the men of Ephraim had refused to do in the past. They were begging Jesus to be in oneness with Him—because that's what the primary distinguishing feature of covenant is. It's unity, oneness, communion.

That's why people were healed: they became one with the Healer. They were in unity with the Son of God who, though He bore our sin and diseases, those things cannot reside in Him.

But Jesus, in allowing people to touch the hem of His garment—the fringe of His prayer shawl—was also healing history. He was healing the historical rift caused by the massacre of the men of Ephraim.

Now Jephthah's warriors, the men of Gilead who were guarding the fords of the Jordan, weren't in fact making a huge demand of the invaders. The twelve tribes, in theory, were already in covenantal submission to one another, so this request merely asked for reaffirmation of brotherhood. Certainly there may have been an implication of an inferior and a superior in the covenantal relationship because, after all, you have to stoop to grasp someone's hem, but it was still about life and blessing and reconciliation.

However, the men of Ephraim would have none of this 'shibboleth' business. They would only say, 'sibboleth,' with its overtones of *carrying a heavy burden*. In effect, they were saying that the people of Gilead should submit to them, be their servants, take on the load and carry them across the river.

Covenantal submission is mutual. It's totally different from the one-sided deference that has come to be associated with our modern understanding of the concept. The Hebrew term for *submission* is almost diametrically opposed in sense to the Greek word from which we derive our present understanding. Both have a sense of *being under*, but in Hebrew this position is for the purpose of *lifting up*. The Greek on the other hand has the sense of being *pressed down*.[17]

Support is an entirely different focus to that of suppression. Covenantal submission looks to mutual uplift and upbuilding, not to a master-servant relationship. Covenantal submission is what Paul encourages us to exhibit when he says: 'Submit to the governing authorities' and 'Wives, submit to your husbands.' It's about *lifting up*, not about being *dominated*.

But this is exactly the kind of submission some people resist with all their might. Like the men of Ephraim insisting on 'Sibboleth,' they'd rather die than give up their sense of superiority. But this kind of submission is also exactly what we need in order to be able to pass the threshold into our calling with its fiery darts and barrage of missiles. This is the submission of a soldier to his paraclete: the mutual support and shielding that comes from being armoured by one who has our covenantal defence at heart.

In mutual uplift and cooperative upbuilding there is no room for pride, for self-sabotage through dishonour, for self-inflicted offence that protects us from examining our own sense of guilt with regard to our failings.

The men of Ephraim were unwilling to repent. They were called by the pledges between the tribal brotherhood and the obligations of covenant to defend the weak or those attacked in war. They chose to ignore those responsibilities. On the banks of the Jordan—a threshold, it should be noted, between their own clan territory and that of Gilead, perhaps even at the very spot overlooked by the town of Jabesh that had been destroyed for doing exactly what they'd done—they simply reiterated their stance. It hadn't changed and the curses of covenant violation descended on them.

When God asks us to reaffirm covenant with Him, He wants us to stoop to touch the hem of Jesus' garment, to humble ourselves in order to receive His blessings and to uplift His name in praise. He does not want us to demand that He should carry us across the threshold, as if He is our servant. Certainly He *is* willing to carry us across the threshold as the Bridegroom, but that is because of His protective love. And yes, He is our servant, but we are not His masters. Rather we are His servants, as He is ours. We are mutual servants, and if we do not understand that, then we cannot belong to Him and know Him, know Him and give Him our loyal allegiance in covenantal oneness as our King.

Prayer

As always in the books in this series, the prayers provided are not meant as a formula but as a starting point. Sometimes, at the end of a chapter, you may realise you've got exactly the problem outlined—but you don't know where to begin to talk to God about it. That's why the prayers are there—to help overcome those initial blockages. Please use them that way, not as an end in themselves.

Lord God and loving Abba,

I hold on by faith to the hem of the garment of Jesus, the fringe of His prayer shawl, the tzitzit of His tallit, and I acknowledge Him as my king. I declare He is Lord of all, including Lord of time and that He is the redeemer of wasted opportunities, wasted years, wasted blessings, wasted finances. I've misused so much of all You've given me to steward, Lord. I've made life about my comfort and my convenience and not about my calling. I have abandoned my purpose in life.

I've been afraid. Afraid of many things. Afraid of You. Please forgive me for allowing fear to rule me and to dictate my relationship with You. I've been like Elijah, unable to face my fear. So just as he ran to the mountain of God, so I've run to the places where I can hide close enough to You to feel safe. I've let myself think that going to Your mountain is going to You, but it's not. Please forgive me for choosing the things associated with You that are not You. I repent of my false refuge and I ask Jesus, the One whose prayer shawl I am holding by faith, to empower that repentance so I choose You as my refuge in the future, nothing and no one else.

Lord, forgive me for my pride in devising my own war plans against the satan and for not following the strategy of Your angel, War. Forgive me for not holding on to the gains that Your heavenly hosts have won for me. Forgive me for my complicity with the spirit of wasting and for failing to align myself with Your purposes. Forgive me for not following Jesus but deviating from the path He has made for me and not choosing to return to it until I've had to be rescued from going my own way. Forgive me for wandering off the path, yet again, almost as soon as I've got back on it.

Forgive me for my lack of patience and my dishonour in choosing Your gifts over You. Forgive me for valuing the Gifts of Your Spirit over the Fruit. Forgive me for my pride in seeking the power gifts and not the more excellent way of love. Forgive me for my reluctance to call on Jesus to increase my faith.

Lord, I repent of my waywardness, my impatience, my disrespect, my wasting, my ambition—without

Your help in empowering my repentance, it's all just bluster and hypocrisy. Help me to be authentic in my desire to please You.

In the name of Jesus of Nazareth.

Amen

2

The Do-Nothing

The world is too much with us, late and soon,
Getting and spending, we waste our powers.

William Wordsworth,
The World Is Too Much With Us

PASSIVITY.

The problem of passivity starts in Eden.

> *When the woman saw that the tree produced good food, was attractive in appearance, and was desirable for making one wise, she took some of its fruit and ate it. Then she also gave some to her husband **who was with her**, and he ate some, too.*[18]

Genesis 3:6 ISV

Adam is with Eve when the tricksy serpent began to sow doubt in her mind about God's goodness and truthfulness. But Adam does nothing and says nothing. He does not correct her statement that God has forbidden even *touching* the tree in the middle of the garden nor does he say to the serpent, 'All very interesting. But God might have an explanation. Do you mind if we chat to Him about this when He turns up? He usually swings by in the cool of the evening.'

Granted, Adam may have been mesmerised since the serpent was an enchanter[19] but, irrespective of that, God still held him primarily responsible for the first sin. His silence and his inaction had consequences for all of humanity. His was the first sin of omission—not doing something that should have been done. Eve's was the first sin of commission—doing something that should not have been done.

Passivity in leaders, particularly when abuse is involved, has dire repercussions.

David's passivity when his eldest son, crown prince Amnon, abused and raped his half-sister Tamar led to civil war, as the nation reaped what David had sown in his adultery with Bathsheba.[20] Abraham's passivity with regards to his wife's abuse of her servant Hagar resulted in centuries of slavery for his descendants, as they reaped what he has sown.

It may seem strange to attribute the servitude of the Israelites under the Egyptians back to Abraham, but that's to miss the clues. During a twilight covenant ceremony, God declared to him:

> 'Know for certain that for four hundred years your descendants will be **strangers** in

> *a country not their own and that they will be **enslaved** and **mistreated** there. But I will punish the nation they serve as slaves, and afterward they will come out with great possessions.'*[21]

Genesis 15:13-14 NIV

This is an enormously strange clause to insert into a covenant agreement. Blessings for keeping covenant, curses for violating it—these were the norm. We've lost any sense of how peculiar this statement is, and thus fail to realise it's supposed to raise a question in our minds: what did Abraham do to cause such a terrible future to be decreed for his descendants?

The answer is not long coming. In fact, the answer is immediate. As soon as God finishes speaking, the story introduces us to Hagar. She is described with the very same words that God used to declare the future of Abraham's family—*mistreated, enslaved*. She's an Egyptian and one possible meaning of her name is *the stranger*.

And so we learn that Sarah's abuse of Hagar didn't start when she became pregnant. It was already so horrific that God makes it clear He will not negotiate with Abraham on the matter, as He did on the fate of Sodom and Gomorrah. He declares it will happen *'for certain'*; there is no appeal.

Passivity is often associated with a lack of initiative, but such a lack is not Abraham's weakness. He's unwilling to confront his wife. He's reluctant to make changes, so the abuse intensifies. He may not be indifferent to Hagar's suffering but, due to his inaction, he may as well be. Eventually he slow-slides from passive complicity with abuse into active abuse.

When he goes to Gerar, he convinces Sarah to go through with a routine they'd enacted once before in Egypt. In fear that he'll be killed because of Sarah's beauty, he gets her to agree to say she's his sister and conceal the fact she's also his wife. Now, back in Egypt, the first time they'd pulled off this stunt, a plague broke out as a result of the deception. So, quite apart from putting Sarah herself in harm's way, Abraham was willing to sacrifice the lives of the people of Gerar to possible plague. He knows what happened in Egypt and he's willing for others to die and for his wife to be molested in order to save his own skin.

By the time Abraham went to Gerar, he had multiple covenants with God—but it's obvious he doesn't believe God will honour them. His refuge is not in the Lord, but in his own disingenuous plan.

In a later age, David is given the task of healing this blot on history. Once again, for the first time since the era of Abraham and Isaac, we hear of a Philistine ruler named Abimelech. At least, that's what David calls him in Psalm 34, though his actual name was Achish, king of Gath. David deceived him, just as Abraham deceived an earlier Abimelech. David was rewarded for his deception, just as Abraham was. But David went further than Abraham—whereas Abraham was merely willing to sacrifice people to cover his deception, David actually did so. He killed all the inhabitants of the towns he raided, making sure there was no survivors who could report to Achish that he was blatantly lying about the locations he was attacking.

The wasted opportunities in this generational saga are immense. Abraham was given a second chance and an opening to redo the test he had failed in Egypt. All it would have taken was for him to trust God and speak the truth to Abimelech of Gerar. But he failed again. God arranged for a third chance when the test passed down to Isaac. He too went to Gerar but once again, like his father, he could not trust God. Abraham had been deceptive in saying Sarah was his sister and concealing she was his wife. He'd given out a half-truth. Isaac, however, in repeating his father's line, told an outright lie. Rebekah was his cousin, not his sister.

God arranged for a fourth chance. But David compounded the failure of Abraham and Isaac by adding massacre to the situation. He then narrowly avoided covenant violation because Achish released him from his commitment to serve as his bodyguard for life. Fortunately for David the other Philistine kings objected to the presence of Hebrew mercenaries in their army. Unfortunately, David chose that moment to ignore his other covenant obligations—to Jonathan and Saul—even though he knew the Philistine objective.

David then proceeded to do what Adam did—indirectly blame God. On arriving back home, he discovered his wives had been taken and the families of his men kidnapped. Now there are times when it's necessary to consult God but a decision whether or not to mount a rescue and retrieve an entire camp of wives and children isn't one of them. Yet David called for the ephod and did so. He was in an invidious position: he could break covenant with Saul and Jonathan or he could break faith with his men. By consulting God, he could always say in the future: 'It wasn't *my* decision.'

Sooner or later, complicity with the spirit of wasting leads to blame of God, whether direct or indirect.

David found himself in a double bind, a self-created one. Double binds are a tactic of Belial, the spirit of abuse, and a perfect complement to wasting. There are two kinds of double binds we encounter in life:

- the type we wrap ourselves into, under the illusion we're cocooning ourselves in safety. Having chained ourselves down, we secure the padlock and throw away the key so that, even if we change our minds, we can't undo the binds.

- the type externally imposed by someone in authority to whom we're accountable. Unless that person is willing to release us from at least one of the constraints they've put in place, we're in danger of losing our calling.

In the saga of the legendary Irish hero Cú Chulainn, a double bind leads to the champion's death. Cú Chulainn has two 'geasa' or binding oaths that involve a taboo: first, he must never eat dog, and second, he must never refuse an invitation to a feast. He's cursed if he breaks either 'geas'. His enemies trap him by putting him in a position where he's forced him to violate his vow. They invite him to a feast where only dog is on the menu. His death follows not long after.

Both his identity and destiny were tied up with dogs and feasts because they were integral to his name. Cú Chulainn means *hound of Chulainn*, and Chulainn was the *lord of the feast*. Two elements of Cú Chulainn's name were thus pitted in a double bind against each other. Other examples of 'geasa' in legend show it can be interpreted as a spoken word that holds a person hostage to the power within their own name.

Leaving aside externally imposed double binds for the moment, let's look at some Scriptural examples of internal, self-created double binds.

Elijah:

- He did not want to confront Jezebel or the spirits that she had invoked.
- He did not want to give up his calling as a prophet.

At Mount Horeb, God had basically told him he could retire so long as he completed three anointings—Elisha as his successor, Jehu and Hazael as kings of Israel and Aram respectively. But it seems Elijah didn't want to retire. But neither did he want to face Jezebel or the young lions she'd called up. Therefore he put off completing his last assignment. He procrastinated, like so many of us do, in the hope that the situation would change and the problem of Jezebel would simply evaporate. But God had made him responsible for changing the government and thereby removing Jezebel. If he went ahead and did that, he would also have to hand over to his successor. It was a package deal. So he did nothing.

Elisha:

- He knew about the unfinished assignment of Elijah and apparently did not want it to remain unfulfilled.
- He apparently could not face the issue of the Gentiles seeking the word of Yahweh while the kings of Israel sought the counsel of Beelzebub.

Like Elijah, he did not anoint Hazael, even though he actually met with him while in Damascus. Hazael had come to Elisha, seeking the counsel of Yahweh on behalf of the king of Aram. Elisha wept during that encounter but did not take the opportunity to introduce a man he knew would be the next king to Yahweh. Imagine a king anointed and blessed by Yahweh and therefore beholden to Him and not the godlings of Aram. Apparently it was an intolerable thought for Elisha.

Likewise he does not preach about Yahweh to the army commander Naaman who was so incredibly open to learning about God after being healed of leprosy.

Also like Elijah, Elisha seems to have resisted the idea of Jehu's appointment to the throne of Israel. Elisha waited until Hazael was king in Aram before sending one of the sons of the prophets to anoint Jehu. Between 21 and 37 years had then elapsed after Elijah met with God at Mount Horeb. For all that time, Elisha followed Elijah's example and did nothing about changing the government.

Jonah:

Jonah is identified in Jewish writing as the anonymous fast runner who was commissioned by Elisha to go anoint Jehu and then hightail it out of the army camp as quickly as he could. He was allegedly a member of the company of prophets, under the tutelage of his mentor, Elisha. I believe this identification is correct because, when Jesus is in the process of handing over Elijah's mantle to Peter, He repeatedly calls him, 'Simon, son of Jonah.'[22]

This therefore means that the story of Jonah's prophetic mission to Nineveh occurs during the reign of Jehu, a century before the rise of the Assyrian empire. God is trying to nip in the bud a merciless, ruthless power before it arrived on the world stage. But Jonah, like Elijah, runs away from the task God has given him. The double bind that precipitates his flight is:

- He does not want God to be merciful to Nineveh.
- He does not want to disobey the God of Israel.

Therefore he leaves Israel, the land chosen by Yahweh, for a nation at the ends of the earth. He sets sail for a place where he believes he will no longer be under the jurisdiction of Yahweh.

If Jonah had introduced the people of Nineveh to Yahweh, then the rise of Assyria—at least as a cruel and pitiless power—may well have been prevented. That, in retrospect, was clearly God's plan. Assyria would then not have warred against Israel and dispersed the ten tribes amongst the nations. However, since the prophets refused to proclaim Yahweh as a light to the Gentiles and a blessing to the nations, then when war inevitably came, the people who knew Yahweh would be dispersed throughout the world—to be light and salt, despite the disobedience of the heralds of God.

Abraham:

As we've seen, Abraham remains quiescent observing the abuse of his second wife by his first. Had he said no when Sarah suggested her servant Hagar could bear him a child in Sarah's name, several thousand years of conflict would have been avoided. His double bind:

- He did not want trouble with Sarah. Perhaps he didn't want to provoke her jealousy further by protecting Hagar. She already blamed him for her servant's uppity attitude.
- He apparently did not want to make things worse for Hagar or the child she was carrying by protecting her.

Therefore he did nothing and became at first passively complicit with abuse, then later actively complicit. God pronounced judgment on Abraham by declaring his descendants through Sarah would suffer mistreatment and slavery, along with rejection as strangers in a foreign land. This divine prophecy spoke to the very conduct Abraham and Sarah had meted out to Hagar and Ishmael.

David:

David has so many self-created double binds it's hard to know where to start.

- He has a covenant with Saul, since he was his armour-bearer, and he also had a threshold covenant with Jonathan. These covenants involved pledges of mutual defence—meaning that, if David knew Jonathan was in danger, he was obligated to come to his aid.

- He also has a covenant with Achish—the king he called Abimelech—a Philistine ruler and thus an enemy of Saul. It is similar to the covenant he has with Saul because he was appointed as Achish's bodyguard for life.

None of these covenants were forced on him. He chose to approach the Philistines, knowing full well the cost of protection would be covenantal vows. Now a threshold covenant, the kind David had pledged with Jonathan, involves mutual defence. Having exchanged weapons and thereby symbolically promised they'd defend each other to the death, the covenant would be violated if one of them knows the other is under threat and does not hurry to assist him.

This is precisely what happened when the Philistine armies massed against the Israelites. David was in a quandary with several conflicting covenants to keep. Fortunately he was sent away by Achish and was thus released from one bind. However, he knew the Philistines planned an attack against Saul and his sons. Perhaps he might be excused breaching covenant with Saul on the basis that Saul broke covenant first. But his covenant with Jonathan still stood. And he did nothing towards that obligation. He went home.

And then he was faced with another double bind. The Amalekites had raided the fortress of Ziklag and taken all the families living there. So then his choice was:

- Rescue Jonathan and the people of Israel from the Philistines.
- Rescue his wives and the families of his men from the Amalekites.

Whatever he chose, it was going to be wrong. That's the nature of a double bind. And that's why he asked for the ephod to be brought out, so God could make the choice. Was there another option that would have avoided a double bind? In this case, I think there was: he could have sent all of his men after the families while he went alone to help Jonathan. That would have fulfilled both obligations.

Later, when he's king, his eldest son Amnon rapes his half-sister Tamar. Again David is caught in a double bind of his own making.

- He would be a hypocrite to discipline Amnon.
- He does not know what to do about Tamar.[23]

Having raped Bathsheba, his much-vaunted righteousness would be contested if he punished Amnon. (I conclude he raped Bathsheba because we reap what we sow, and rape was the collateral consequence of God's pronunciation that the sword would never depart from David's house. Both David's daughter and ten of his concubines were raped, Tamar's violation indirectly sparking the civil war that pitted Absalom against his father.) But, in neither consoling Tamar nor establishing a way forward for her, David so enraged Absalom that he vowed vengeance against his older brother and his father.

David did nothing, dispensing neither justice towards Amnon nor mercy towards Tamar. In later doing nothing once again, after Absalom killed Amnon and then fled for three years before returning to Jerusalem, David allowed the brooding clouds of civil war to foment.

David's choice to wash his hands of various unpleasant matters and thereby try to divest himself of responsibility is reminiscent of the actions of Pontius Pilate. In fact, John's gospel directly compares both men. At two different historical junctures, a group of people met with the ruler of Jerusalem requesting permission to put innocent men to death at the Passover. In each case, the ruler gave his consent. David breached covenant in granting his approval, while Pilate violated the laws of Roman jurisprudence.

During David's reign, the Gibeonites said to him:

> *'It's not for us to execute anyone in Israel.'*
>
> 2 Samuel 21:4 ISV

During the governorship of Pontius Pilate, the chief priests said to him:

'We are not permitted to execute anyone.'
John 18:31 BSB

The words are almost identical. David, it transpires, was—depending on the circumstances—just as wishy-washy and weak-willed as Pilate was.

All of these choices to 'do-nothing' on the part of the patriarchs, prophets and kings had dire long-term consequences. A decision to do nothing is just as much a decision as one to do something. Yet a resolve to do nothing cedes control of the situation to the spirit of wasting. We might dither and hesitate and feel guilty about doing nothing, but unless we change and stop procrastinating, then we are responsible for any ruin that results. Yet, that's not to say we should go to the opposite extreme and wear ourselves out with busily fixing every aspect of the crisis we can. That's putting ourselves into the hands of the spirit of wasting in a different way. If we're too exhausted to be able to process an unfolding situation with wisdom and discernment, then we'll simply fall into a different trap set by the same spirit. It doesn't matter if we're sitting still doing nothing or running around frantically doing everything, we're just as complicit with Rachab.

We need to be waiting on God, listening closely for His voice to know the moment to act once we've decided on the choice to enact.

Thresholds are testing places. Generally speaking, God is silent—because it's our choice, not His. He's not the one being tested, we are. Just as Adam and Eve were tested with a choice, so are we. We can ask God questions about the choice, but most of the time He won't tell us what choice to make. We have to decide for ourselves amongst the options presented to us which one is the most loving, the most truthful and the most just, as well as which one will express our loyalty to God and which one is most in keeping with our belief in the atonement of Jesus. We are not to sacrifice others, ourselves or the honour of God. Nor are we to sabotage others, ourselves or the honour of God.

We can *make* a sacrifice but should not *be* a sacrifice. Jesus is already our all-sufficient offering. Anything we try to add denies the perfection of His atonement.

When it comes to dealing with the spirit of wasting, we need to consider two different generational aspects of any complicity as well as any cooperation of our own with Rachab.

In addition to any corruption of our bloodline, we also need to consider the defilement of our faithline.

Faithline.

Believers often forget that we belong to two families: one of flesh and blood, and one of faith. The sins of our physical and adoptive forebears impact our bloodline while the sins of our forerunners in the faith affect our faithline.

Just as we have to forgive our ancestors for their transgressions, and sometimes repent as well, so too we have to forgive our predecessors in the faith for their transgressions and repent where necessary. You might think to yourself that it is pointless, inappropriate, disrespectful and utterly bizarre to talk about forgiving David, for example. You may well consider that his misdeeds are so far back in history they cannot possibly affect us today. Sorry to burst your bubble but the past is not gone, it is here with us.

Look around and observe the renowned leaders who have openly modelled themselves on David. Note their fall into sexual sin; their inaction regarding abuse; the way they've set up those who work under them so that their personal ministries, if not their lives, are killed off; their deception regarding property; their ever-expanding building projects; their willingness to sacrifice others to advance their own agendas. They've followed the profile of David a little too exactly.

Look at those who claim to be experiencing an Abrahamic journey and see the slide from toleration of abuse to cult-like coercive control.

Look at those who say they've been told they have an Elijah mantle and ask them if they were on fire for the Lord twenty years ago but haven't done anything much ever since.

The past is *now.* And when that is the case, we know that we need to treat a faithline like a bloodline and subject it to the transformative work of repentance, renunciation and forgiveness through the power of the Cross.

Prayer

Loving Abba Father,

May Your name be always holy, set apart, uplifted and glorified. I have not always done that. I have been complicit with the spirit of wasting and blamed You, not always directly but indirectly and implicitly. I've been like Adam and accepted fear as my master and so looked for some way to deflect my distress. I've flipped my shame back to you as blame; and Jesus has taken that shame to the Cross but I'm still too scared to enter the glory He's won for me.

I've been, not just like Adam, but like Elijah, Elisha, Jonah, Abraham and David. I've been passive. I've been in agreement with 'doing nothing' not just for days and weeks but for months and years. I just wanted You to sort the issues without input from me. I've pretended the problems didn't exist in the hope they'd just disappear or somehow resolve themselves if I waited long enough. 'Wait on the Lord,' I've told myself, refusing to face my own hypocrisy. I've accepted a double bind of my own devising to allay the fear of getting too close to You and hearing You tell me

I need to take responsibility and take up the hard and unpleasant task of working through the mess.

Lord, I recognise that my faults are not unique to me. They come down a faithline from Adam, Abraham, David, Elijah, Elisha and Jonah to name just a few. I forgive those ancestors of mine in the family of faith who role-modelled to me passivity, conflict avoidance and complicity with wasting. I ask Jesus, my mediator before You, to add in any names in my faithline or bloodline to whom this forgiveness should be extended and I ask Him, by the power of His atoning blood, to give life and activation to my words of forgiveness. I also ask that He empower my repentance as I ask Him to transform my mind and my heart so that I am willing to have Him remove the double binds of my own making and help me through the panic and fear that will come when they are cut away.

Lord, help me to fix my eyes on Jesus, to look only to Him—not to lower my gaze and follow one of the great, but flawed, heroes of the Bible. Help me to know, to *really* know, no one is good, except You alone. But that Your unswerving desire is that I become good and in that lifelong process, through the power of Your covenantal love, be always and forever an instrument of Your good.

In the name of Jesus of Nazareth.

Amen

3

Atonement and Covenant

In the world's finale, at the moment of eternal harmony, something so precious will come to pass that it will suffice for all hearts, for the comforting of all resentments, for the atonement of all the crimes of humanity, for all the blood that they've shed; that it will make it not only possible to forgive but to justify all that has happened.

Fyodor Dostoevsky
The Brothers Karamazov

What does *atonement* mean?

It's such a critical word throughout this book that it's important we understand the basic idea. Atonement, fortunately for us in the English-speaking world, spells out its own nature: at one ment. It's the state of being *at one*, or *in oneness*, with another person. It refers to reconciliation after betrayal, to reunion after separation, to reconnection after estrangement.

The death of Jesus on the Cross was the means of atonement for the sin of Adam and for also the entire cascade of iniquity that followed throughout the ages. It is all-sufficient, meaning that nothing can or needs to be added to it to bring humanity back into relationship with God. That's not to say that God has flicked some cosmic switch and decided everyone is, by default, now back in covenantal oneness with Him. There's a small condition before the Light can be turned on. To make it as simple as possible so that even a tiny child can be part of His family, all God requires is faith in Jesus. Fortunately He requires no more to begin than a crumb of trust, a mote of belief no bigger than a mustard seed, or we'd be no better off than before.

The all-sufficiency of the atonement means that, with Jesus' help, we can resist every temptation and put every sinful habit behind us. We can demolish the false refuges in our lives and we can receive the fullness of covenantal defence that is an aspect of our inheritance in Christ. Salvation is ours in all its completeness: healing, health, recompense, restitution, justice, wholeness, integrity, prosperity—that is, having enough for our daily needs and enough left over to be generous. We'll be able to enter our calling and achieve the destiny that God has for us and we'll be able to don the mantle that we've been given as a divine inheritance and advance the assignment that it carries towards complete fulfillment.

So why does it all go so very wrong?

Partly because we don't fully believe in the atonement and our lack of faith restricts our access to it. Partly because the forces of the satan have, over the centuries, devised an entire range of successful strategies to deceive us into believing that access to the atonement is simply a matter of *more* faith when often it's a matter of repentance, forgiveness and Fruit.[24] And partly because, even when we finally realise that partial commitment to Jesus is actually no commitment at all, the enemy of our souls still has a few tricks up his sleeve. And because he relies heavily on our ignorance of covenant—an ignorance he's aided and abetted over the last century and a half—he's generally successful.

A friend remarked recently on a comment I made in *Spiritual Legal Rights II* about the fact I used to be surprised that, whenever I asked anyone who'd been in counselling for decades whether they'd ever had prayer ministry for ungodly covenants in relation to ritual abuse, the answer was invariably no. She commented that, now she's started to look out for it as she has progressed through various training courses, she's noticed it's a topic never addressed.

Covenants are our spiritual blind spot. First, we think there's only one kind—the blood covenant—and because God has taken on all of the legal responsibilities for that particular one, then any and all curses have been sorted at the Cross and we don't need to concern ourselves any further.

But the blood covenant is not the only type. There are at least four others.

Second, we've been given the impression that covenants are just like contracts, only more solemn, and they become null and void on the death of one of the oath-takers. In our minds, covenants are limited to those who made the pledges to one another and therefore they simply cease to exist when one of the partners to the agreement passes away. They are, so we think, a bit like marriages—the widow or widower is free to move on, once their spouse is gone.

The truth is quite different. For a start, a covenant is *not* a contract. Yes, it certainly has contractual obligations but it is radically and fundamentally different from a contract. Nor is it limited to the lifetime of those who agree to it. It covers all their descendants in perpetuity—until someone revokes it. And, even when the specific curses for covenant violation are known— and these curses, naturally, cover any attempt to dissolve the covenant—then any renunciation needs to be done with great care and total reliance on Jesus because of the dangers involved.

Third, the most significant difference between a covenant and a contract is oneness. Now, by *oneness*, I certainly don't mean anything akin to the mysticism of the new age movement. There *oneness* refers to the state of being seamlessly at one with the universe, an awareness of union or communion with the earth, a sense of limitlessness, of omnipotence, of being able to create your own reality, of being God. It's a denial of any spiritual barrier between the self and others, nature or God. After all, how can there possibly be any rift between the self and God, if the self *is* God?

There is no sin in this belief system and therefore no need for atonement of any kind. Nor is there any need for reconciliation between humanity and God, humanity and creation or between the self and others. We are allegedly able to live in harmony with all things. We've apparently never been exiled from Eden and the promise of the serpent that we will be *like* God has been made manifest and even surpassed—we *are* God.

That's NOT the kind of oneness I'm referring to when I speak of covenantal oneness. Covenantal oneness is born of reconciliation with God—it's a return to union after separation. It's a joining with Him that has only been made possible through the power of the atonement of Jesus. It's rebirth, it's marriage and it's tabernacling. It's dwelling in Him as He dwells in us.

It's NOT the kind of oneness where our individuality is swallowed up in cosmic vastness, even nothingness, but rather it's a oneness that treasures individuality as necessary to the proper functioning of the Body. Each of us has different gifts that we are to bring together to create *symphony*, the word Jesus uses when He says that wherever two or three *agree* in His name, whatever they ask for will be done for them.[25]

Now in our misunderstanding of both oneness and covenant, we're apt to think that there can be only one kind of oneness. But there are several different sorts. The oneness of marriage, for example, is not the same as the oneness of family. Just as there are different kinds of onenesses, there are different kinds of covenant that take account of these onenesses.

- BLOOD covenant
- NAME covenant
- THRESHOLD covenant
- SALT covenant
- PEACE covenant

And, of course, there's the NEW covenant that Jesus instituted on the night before He died. It combines all of the above as well as marriage. It may seem strange that marriage is not in the list but that's because it's also a mix of several other covenants.

Now it's quite likely you may not have heard of all these different types. Most people have heard of blood and salt covenants but the others are usually unfamiliar. Threshold covenant, in particular, is a complete unknown to many people but it is in fact the most common and also the most famous of all, since it is commemorated at the Passover. It is also called *cornerstone* covenant, covenant of *hospitality* and covenant of *defence*. It appears to be the same as the covenant of *freedom* described in Jeremiah 34:15.

Now, theologically speaking, over the last century and a half, all these different covenants have been subsumed under BLOOD covenant. In erasing the others—NAME, THRESHOLD, SALT and PEACE—there's been a failure to understand the process of sanctification. Our relationship with God is meant to mature over time and move on from one level to another. A BLOOD covenant brings us into the family of God and makes us His children. That's not a status we can lose. A divine BLOOD covenant says to the world: 'We are one family. Jesus is my Brother, God is my Father.' We won't cease to be God's child at any point in the future—therefore our salvation, which is one of the blessings of BLOOD covenant, is secure.

In a BLOOD covenant with God, all the obligations and responsibilities are His. He promises us all the blessings and reserves the curses to Himself. Just as Abraham was asleep when God cut a blood covenant with him,[26] so we are 'asleep', dead in our sins, when He covenants with us to bring us into His family and call us His child.

However, just as not every child becomes a friend of their parents, so not every child of God goes on to raise a NAME covenant with Him and become His friend. When God proposes a NAME covenant, the obligations become mutual. We're awake now, after all. We've hopefully grown in maturity and our faith has weathered several crises and come out stronger. So now it's time for us to move on from childhood and shoulder our responsibilities. When God calls us to be His friend, it's because we've demonstrated loyalty and commitment to Him. This is important for our own safety because friendship changes the dynamic. For the first time, treachery is possible. Enemies don't betray, friends do. And because the obligations are now mutual, betrayal has terrible consequences. A divine NAME covenant says to the world: 'We are one in friendship. Our hearts, souls and minds are knit together.' A NAME covenant involves an exchange of names—we tend to notice when Abram becomes Abraham or Simon becomes Cephas, but it's easy to miss that there's a revelation of a new name for God in these stories as well: 'El Shaddai' accompanies 'Abraham', and 'Messiah' accompanies 'Cephas' (or 'Peter').[27]

We may have to wait years between BLOOD covenant and NAME covenant. Abraham waited nearly fourteen. But God now proposes a rapid succession of covenantal undertakings. Six days after a NAME covenant with God, He'll institute a THRESHOLD covenant and SALT covenant. A THRESHOLD covenant—also known as a CORNERSTONE covenant—involves HOSPITALITY and constitutes an agreement of mutual DEFENCE. It's like saying: 'You and I are one when either of us is attacked. I will defend you as if I'm defending myself. I will come to your aid and fight to the death on your behalf.' This is the covenant that existed between David and Jonathan. It is also the basis of the Passover ritual of painting blood on the lintels and doorposts that would drip down onto the CORNERSTONE. The blood was an invitation to a guest that a feast had been prepared to welcome them and, so long as they were willing to accept the covenant of DEFENCE, all they had to do was *pass over* the CORNERSTONE without touching the blood.[28]

Hospitality was so significant in the ancient world that, even outside of Israel where no covenant was involved, the obligations of mutual defence were paramount. In Greece, 'xenia' or *guest friendship* was understood as a moral responsibility and a political imperative, particularly towards foreigners.[29] It entailed generosity, gift-giving, protection and shelter. While *oneness* might not have been involved, reciprocity was expected—that is, mutual honour was foundational. That is why when Paris, a prince of Troy, broke the rules of 'xenia' and absconded with Helen, the wife of his host, that the decade-long Trojan War erupted. It wasn't just about the revenge of an abandoned husband, but about the prospect of complete societal breakdown if punishment for violating 'xenia' was not enforced. People had to be able to offer hospitality without fear the guest would ruin their lives.

A SALT covenant guarantees the permanency of the other covenants. David had a SALT covenant with God but, as we shall see, it didn't mean what he thought it did. Unless God specifies unconditionality—and, in David's case, He clearly stipulated obedience as a requirement for a throne that would stand firm through all generations—then the precondition for permanency is keeping the covenantal clauses.

The covenant of PEACE is so rare that—apart from Jesus—only the high priest Phinehas ever seems to have been granted it. It comes from a willingness to be one with a curse. Jesus has already fulfilled this on our behalf. A THRESHOLD covenant occurs when we accept God's invitation to be our Covenant Defender against the threshold guardians who would otherwise be continually triumphant over us as we try to enter our calling. A covenant of PEACE occurs when we accept God's invitation to act on His behalf as the covenant defenders of others.

Now because of the theological crushing of all covenants into a singularity—the BLOOD covenant—we are more likely than not to misunderstand God when He presents us with other covenant offers. I've turned down both NAME covenant and the covenant of PEACE, not realising how necessary they are in the battles of life. Also because of the covenant-crushing, we entirely miss the importance of faithfulness to God as our response to grace. We are saved by grace through faith but, unless our faith produces faithfulness, we'll be forever on a diet of milk, not meat. We'll be babies, not adults who have demonstrated by a constancy of devotion that we are safely able to be friends with God. And without the Name covenant closely followed by the Threshold covenant, we'll be unable to get into our calling.

Each one of these covenants looks to different jewel-like dimensions of the atonement of Jesus and the oneness He won for us.

I find it beyond strange that none of the seven theories of the atonement[30]—Recapitulation, Ransom, Satisfaction, Penal-substitution, Moral Example, Christus Victor, Christian Universalist—even remotely addresses these different facets. It's as if atonement has been stripped of its different at_one_ments and the extravagant glory of what Christ achieved on the Cross is flattened and compressed into a single dimension and most of its light extinguished.

Atonement and covering are intrinsically related. The Hebrew word, 'kaphar', means both *cover* and *atone*. This, as we shall see, has immense ramifications.

Covenants are so speechlessly amazing—what a paltry word 'amazing' is to describe them—that it's no surprise the enemy of our souls has gone all-out to defile each and every divine pact. In addition, he has wily strategies to lure us away from God through counterfeit covenants. These unholy covenants purport to offer benefits just as good as God's and, to clinch the deal, they do not have any conditions about remaining faithful attached to them.[31]

One of the reasons the threshold guardians demand a sacrifice in order to pass through the entryway into our calling is because a sacrifice made at a threshold constitutes a covenant. Until the late nineteenth century this was common knowledge in the west—it remains so in some parts of the Middle East—but the satan has done such a good job of depriving us of the knowledge of good and evil that he can rely on our ignorance to pull us into his orbit. As we push on through the doorway into our calling that we can see God has opened wide for us, disaster often strikes because, on the threshold, we made a covenant with the enemy, thinking it was with God.

Two of the most common ungodly covenants are with Death and with the grave. Isaiah describes them in his prophecy, connecting their establishment to false refuges[32] and their overturning to the cornerstone laid in Zion. He addresses the rulers who have become so terrified of the Assyrians, they have abandoned God and looked for spiritual rescue elsewhere:

> *Therefore hear the word of the Lord, O scoffers who rule this people in Jerusalem. For you said, 'We have made a covenant with Death; we have fashioned an agreement with Sheol. When the overwhelming scourge passes through it will*

> *not touch us, because we have made lies our refuge and falsehood our hiding place.'*
>
> *So this is what the Lord God says: 'See, I lay a stone in Zion, a tested stone, a precious cornerstone, a sure foundation; the one who believes will never be shaken.*
>
> *I will make justice the measuring line and righteousness the level. Hail will sweep away your refuge of lies, and water will flood your hiding place. Your covenant with Death will be dissolved, and your agreement with Sheol will not stand.*
>
> Isaiah 28:14–18 BSB

A covenant with Death is only possible when we've lost all faith in God as our covenant defender. We choose what Ted Peters calls 'unfaith'—to distinguish it from *doubt* which is a struggle between belief and unbelief. As we shall see, unfaith is the second step down the ladder into the practice of evil.

A covenant with Death is *not* a death wish. Quite the contrary. A lot of people confuse the two, but a death wish is an embrace of the idea of dying, whereas a covenant with Death is a total rebuff of that idea. A covenant with Death comes about because of a desire for survival at any cost, and is a result of a belief that God is not the most powerful being in the universe—allegedly Death is. Therefore people like those rulers in Jerusalem in the time of Isaiah devise a seriously perverted plan: they choose to make a covenant with

Death to protect them from itself. Then, for double insurance, they make an agreement with Sheol, *the grave*, for knowledge as to how to stay alive.

Every covenant involves an exchange and, in these two cases, the trades are simple.

With Death:

- survival is offered in exchange for inheritance. All the family ever gets from one generation to the next is survival, there is no inheritance to pass on.

With Sheol:

- prophetic sight is offered in exchange for knowledge. The seers and those with prophetic giftings in a family line are completely tainted by this covenant.

These covenants do not disappear when those who lost faith in God and allied themselves with His enemy pass away. There is no end-date to these agreements. They keep on keeping on, generation after generation, until they are revoked. But because of the curses attached to the revocation of these covenants, that has to be done with great care under the guidance of the Holy Spirit. You don't just renounce a covenant. You begin by dealing with any false refuges in your life. This is why, at the very start of this book, I recommended you work through *Hidden in the Cleft: True and False Refuge* first.

The covenant with Death is a counterfeit of both the THRESHOLD covenant and the covenant of PEACE. In raising a covenant with Death, people are seeking to buy protection from death. On the other hand, a divine THRESHOLD covenant is God's promise of defence for the individual while the covenant of PEACE is a covering for family, community and ultimately nation.

Now God has set up for us, in addition to these covenants, other protective measures. His armour, as described in Ephesians 6:10–18, is specifically given to us for the crossing of thresholds as is evidenced by the multiple puns in the Greek language involving parts of a doorway.[33] This armour is, with the single exception of the sword of the Word of God, defensive in nature. However, God has also given us armaments that we can deploy against the enemy.

These weapons are wondrous: we can ignite them and set them off and they'll do no harm to us whatsoever but they'll scatter the enemy far and wide. They are, however, very narrow in their effectiveness. What works against Python won't work against Ziz and what works against Leviathan won't work against Belial or Lilith.

This set of armaments is the Fruit of the Spirit and, throughout this series, its applicability to each of the threshold spirits has been detailed. In Eden, fruit was weaponised against humanity by our adversary. So now, by the principle of sowing-and-reaping, the

Fruit of the Spirit has become weaponry against our spiritual opponents.

LOVE is effective against Python.

JOY is effective against Ziz.

PEACE—'shalom'—is effective against Leviathan.

KINDNESS, GOODNESS and FAITHFULNESS—'chesed'—is effective against Belial.

GENTLENESS—*meekness, strength under control*—is effective against Lilith.

SELF-CONTROL—*Spirit-empowerment*—is effective against Azazel.

And last but, by no means least, PATIENCE is effective against Rachab.

Remember that God's Terror, the angel called War, has a tactical plan to drive out wasting—but it will be a slow, thorough process.

One of the greatest strategists in the German military of World War II was the commanding general, Erwin Rommel—he was able to smash through enemy lines, taking huge swathes of territory. But, because of his singular blind spot—always advancing way too far beyond his supply lines—he was constantly forced to retreat and was unable to hold the ground he had won.

The angel, War, does not make this elementary mistake. When he goes ahead of us, he is intent on ensuring all our gains can be maintained, no wasting occurs, and no power vacuum is created that can be filled by troublesome and opportunistic spirits who spot a vacancy and decide to move in.

As a result of this slowness, PATIENCE is absolutely essential. Our impatience with the process can lead us into disobedience and thus we can undermine all our efforts to that point by putting ourselves back into the hands of the spirit of wasting. However, it's not just impatience that can be a problem. So can too much patience. Too much patience can be a false refuge, a corrupt way of avoiding conflict as we procrastinate about taking needed action.

Wherever I look at the moment, I see an online ad telling me that procrastination is not laziness, it's a depression response. The ad is irritating because it's half-true and it gives the impression it's validating neglect, conflict avoidance or a sustained failure to keep a promise. Depression just as often comes from procrastination, as it happens the other way around. Procrastination is frequently a false refuge.

True, genuine godly PATIENCE does not mean that we wait indefinitely for God to act, to give us a signal or to obey His orders. Early last year, God told me I was to go to a particular town where my mother's mother grew up and do some investigation into my heritage. I waited and waited for Him to tell me when to go. One day when I inquired of Him if the time was right, He told me I should already have gone and come back. Did I miss His signal? No, it turned out there wasn't one. He'd simply given me my own choice within a window of time. Instead I was waiting for a specific sign.

In discovering godly parameters for PATIENCE within any particular situation, we need to inquire of God what the limits should be. When is the time too short? When is the time too long? What is the balance between impatience and overly patient? What is a strategy to negotiate a peaceful path through any potential clash if we're pathological conflict avoiders?

Both PATIENCE and *passion* both come from the same root word, 'patior', *to suffer*. In fact, PATIENCE is often translated *long-suffering*. It refers to a length of time. When God revealed His glory to Moses, He also declared His nature:

> *The Lord, the Lord God, merciful and gracious, longsuffering, and abounding in goodness and truth, keeping mercy for thousands, forgiving iniquity and transgression and sin, by no means clearing the guilty, visiting the iniquity of the fathers upon the children and the children's children to the third and the fourth generation.*
>
> Exodus 34:6–7 NKJV

PATIENCE certainly does not mean we allow others to get away with unloving actions, because PATIENCE is an integral component of LOVE and therefore of covenantal defence.

Love is patient, love is kind. It does not envy, it does not boast, it is not proud. It does not dishonour others, it is not self-seeking, it is not easily angered, it keeps no record of wrongs. Love does not delight in evil but rejoices with the truth. It always protects, always trusts, always hopes, always perseveres. Love never fails.

1 Corinthians 13:4–8 NIV

When the cabal of threshold spirits unites against us to bring us down, we are to deploy the Fruit of the Spirit so we can hold the ground God's angel armies have cleared for us.

Prayer

Loving God,

I don't believe in the atonement of Jesus. If I did have faith in its all-sufficiency, I'd be in my calling, the spirit of wasting would have no power over me, I'd be doing greater things than Jesus every day, I'd love to spend time with You, I'd have no false refuges or ungodly covenants. I'd be utterly surrendered to You.

In addition to not believing in the atonement, I am unwilling to accept that it's pure grace. That there's nothing I can add to it, nothing I can do to help Jesus save me. If I'm good and obey Your commandments, surely that counts. If I sow a seed of faith or gift You regular offerings of time or money, surely that counts. If I forgive, if I repent, if I'm generous, surely that counts. You are no one's debtor, I'm told, but in my dark and secret thoughts I'd really like to find a way to put You in my debt so that I could earn Your favour. I am so uncomfortable knowing that Your grace is undeserved. It makes me feel powerless, vulnerable, uneasy and afraid. How can I depend on something as uncertain as grace?

I see how right Jeremiah was. My heart is indeed desperately wicked and incurably deceitful. It keeps striving to find something to do that will make a difference and earn me more of Your grace. It doesn't want to acknowledge that Your love is enough, that the atonement is sufficient, that Your provision is more than adequate, or that Your covenants are secure and unbreakable—except by me. And that's the problem. I'm weak and tempted and, when it comes to faithfulness, I'm erratic. There are times when I don't even want to be good, I don't want to give up my false refuges, and I don't care if everything goes to waste. There are times when I'm just over all the stresses and strains and disappointments of life. But...

> *This is a faithful saying:*
> *For if we died with Him,*
> *We shall also live with Him.*
> *If we endure,*
> *We shall also reign with Him.*
> *If we deny Him,*
> *He also will deny us.*
> *If we are faithless,*
> *He remains faithful;*
> *He cannot deny Himself.*
>
> 2 Timothy 2:11–13 NKJV

So, in Your faithfulness to me, give me the strength to be faithful, to believe in Your Son's atonement, to accept Your grace without trying to earn it, to well up with gratitude for the oneness You offer with Yourself, to delight in Your covenants and to uplift Your name through all the world.

In the name of Jesus of Nazareth.

Amen

4

Broken Haloes

In 1936, Yezhov became People's Commissar for Internal Affairs (head of the NKVD) and began a purge of Russia's leadership. About half the political and military establishment were killed in the next two years. Automatic guilty verdicts were instated against anyone—and their wives and children over 15—deemed 'socially dangerous'. This included anyone negotiating with or considered influenced by foreign powers. Since the new corps of the Red Army were German-trained, this essentially included all of them. A corps was created with German assistance to train the army against the growing German threat and was then killed for consorting with Germans.

Stephen Weir
History's Worst Decisions and the People Who Made Them

'I CAN'T PRAY FOR YOU.'

Imagine approaching a church leader, a shepherd of the flock, full of anguish and distress. Imagine exposing your wounds and pouring out your heartache to a spiritual overseer and guide, only to be told, 'I can't pray for you.' Imagine the initial numbing shock of hearing such words and then the confusion and added distress they cause.

Several times over the last few decades, different people have approached me because a church leader has turned on them with these devastating words. They had sought help in a crisis but were rebuffed—they were not just sent away without help but without spiritual solace either. Until that moment of refusal, each person I spoke with was utterly convinced the leader was a friend, someone with whom they'd done life together and who could be counted on through thick and thin. The sense of betrayal was acute.

In fact, the resulting emotional and spiritual turmoil meant that any accompanying reasons were impossibly difficult to process. Let me briefly outline some of the situations and the reasons—in reality, excuses—that were given in different circumstances and by different leaders for speaking these five destructive words:

- I'm supporting your wife during this separation, so I can't pray for you to be reconciled.
- I realise you have panic attacks if you leave your home but, unless you demonstrate your

faith by coming to me, I can't pray for you about overcoming them.
- Because of your throat cancer you can't speak and so, since you can't respond, I can't pray for you.
- Your life is too messy to sort through, so I can't pray for you.
- You should just forgive me for not paying for your help on the last project; I've already moved on to my next project and, in fact, I'm so busy at the moment I can't pray for you.

Responses like these constitute violations of the soul. They create externally imposed double binds, completely different from the self-generated double binds mentioned in the last chapter. In withholding prayer, they weaponise it. All of these situations were distinctive in their own way but every one of them, as I eventually came to see, had far more in common than those key words, 'I can't pray for you.'

Jenny (a second Jenny) had called a deliverance minister to come and pray for her husband who was seriously ill with throat cancer. The minister was their friend. Over the years, he'd been so close to her husband that he'd repeatedly called him 'family'. The minister made a time to visit, but the day came and went. As it transpired, he'd forgotten he had another appointment. He set another date, but forgot again and double-booked once more. Another time was arranged, another episode of forgetfulness followed. And another.

Jenny rallied her friends to pray that the minister would actually remember to turn up for the next appointment. *Yes!* The prayer was answered. *Hallelujah!* (Jenny's a very 'hallelujah' kind of person.) He finally came.

But —

Neither Jenny nor her friends thought it necessary to pray beyond getting the minister there. Every one of us automatically assumed that turning up meant a deliverance session would proceed. In retrospect that was naïve. The minister turned up, visited for fifteen minutes, chatted briefly outside the sickroom, then left without even saying goodbye to her husband.

A few days later a text came from him to the effect that, because Jenny's husband couldn't speak clearly, the minister couldn't pray deliverance for him. Jenny was dumbfounded.

She updated me on what had happened and, after I got over my speechless bafflement, I was struck by the conditional nature of the help from someone who'd repeatedly said, 'We're family.' While Jenny and I were trying to process the weirdness of the situation over the phone—first the extreme forgetfulness, then the refusal to pray—somehow I found myself telling her the story of God's miraculous intervention in another situation where 'I can't pray for you' was invoked by a church leader.

I'd got to be the hinge in a two-part decade-long story. My friend Andrew had mysteriously developed agoraphobia. He'd started to have panic attacks as soon as he stepped outside his front gate. He'd asked the leader of his church to come and pray for him, but the pastor and the leadership team made a condition: 'You come to us. You must demonstrate faith for healing.'

This continued for over two years—Andrew made repeated requests for help but was always denied. Andrew's wife would attend services, and so-called friends would speak about him with dishonour. 'How's that lazy husband of yours?' they'd ask.

Andrew was frustrated. 'If I had a broken leg, they'd come and pray for me. But because it's a mental health condition, they won't.' In the third year of his disability, Andrew started looking outside his local congregation for help. He decided to seek deliverance from an entirely different source and so contacted a well-known couple who were willing to come to his home. Unfortunately this couple made inquiries at his church, asking if there was any background information they should know about. Absolutely, as it transpired, there most certainly was. All could have been resolved at this point, if the leadership had thought to give the details of the missionary trip Andrew had been sent on. But all the leadership team said to the couple was: 'Don't go to him. Tell him to come to you.'

So that's what the couple did. Like the church, they made leaving the house a condition of receiving deliverance ministry. It was another impasse for Andrew as he sought healing.

I knew him all through this time and I prayed continually for him. While I agreed that the church should have tested the situation for a few weeks, it should never have progressed to a year, let alone three. Nor should the church leadership have stopped anyone outside from praying. Once it became obvious that Andrew had a genuine problem, the church should have been praying for him, not slapping 'lazy', 'faith-lacking' labels on him to excuse their own inaction.

This is about control. Nothing less than the exercise of raw power. It was vile, degrading and unspeakably ungodly.

The Lord worked on the matter for another seven years. Important to the second half of this story is the fact that neither Andrew nor his wife had ever told me any names. They'd explained what was happening in their church and with the leadership team but, in their care not to dishonour anyone, they had never mentioned who the people were.

I was therefore blissfully ignorant.

Several years later, while I was acting as the review editor for a national women's magazine, I received a self-published book in the mail from a local pastor. I flicked through it, wondering which of the review team I should send it to. A couple of paragraphs caught my attention. 'I don't think that's the right Hebrew word,' I said to myself. I leafed through a few more pages and spotted a few more dubious entries. 'And I don't think that's the right Hebrew word either.'

So I read the entire book myself and came to the conclusion that auto-correct had 'fixed' every single Hebrew word in the text and no one had picked it up in the proof-reading. I wrote a letter to the author, suggesting that, come the second edition, he might like to amend the mistakes. I also offered in passing, if ever he did another book in the future, to proofread it for free.

I was, in fact, seriously indebted to him for all those mistakes. In checking those Hebrew words, I'd found the source of his research and it confirmed for me a very unusual revelation of the Holy Spirit from some time previously about armour, submission, kissing and marriage. I got to work on a book I'd been putting off.[34]

Now I didn't receive any immediate response from the author to my letter. Though I did hear, along the grapevine, through Andrew and his wife, that he'd pulped several thousand copies of the book. I should have suspected they knew the author at this point, I guess, but I didn't. He was a sufficiently well-known name in the national scene for me not to query how they knew. I just laughed at the rumour they passed on—that the reason the book had been consigned to the trash was because it was a mismatch in size with its accompanying study guide. I knew that wasn't right. There were some very big-name endorsements in the book and every single Hebrew word—of which there were many—was wrong. *That* was the reason.

About eighteen months down the track I finally got a return letter from the author, asking me if my offer to proofread his next book was still open. Yes, I said. So several months later I got a new manuscript by email and, on checking it, I responded: 'I have good news and bad news. The good news is that all your Hebrew words are now correct. However, all of your Greek words are wrong.'

'You have no idea how indebted I am to you,' the author wrote. Actually, knowing the cost of a print run and thus being aware of how costly his previous mistake had been, I had a fair idea.

'What do you want?' the author continued.

Whoever asks a question like that? It's a fairytale question. It should never occur in real life. It's the perilous question posed in folklore by a ruler to the hero for curing his daughter or somesuch similar; it's usually bounded by 'up to half my kingdom'; it's Herod's question to Salome after she pleases his guests with her dancing; it's Xerxes' pledge to Esther when he extends his sceptre to her; it's Morden's temptation in the *Babylon 5* series.

'What do I want?' I wondered. I went to God and put it to Him, 'What should I ask for?'

God immediately reminded me that the author was a pastor. He also brought to my attention the fact I'd recently learned from Andrew that his problems had started right after a missionary trip where he'd been given a mantle by the leader in order to carry his authority into the nation he was visiting.

'Why don't you ask him to pray and lift the mantle off Andrew?' God suggested.

'Fabulous idea,' I said to myself, walking straight into the set-up. All Andrew needed in my view was someone with authority to remove the mantle. He'd been getting better lately. He'd been able to walk to the local shops and, even though he was attacked by jitters at times, he'd persisted in trying.

'Can you make it as far as a coffee shop?' I asked him. 'There's this pastor who owes me a favour and I think I could get him to meet with you and pray for that mantle on you to be removed.'

Andrew agreed and a date was set.

The day before the coffee shop appointment I phoned to check if Andrew was still ok to come. In the course of the conversation I happened to mention the pastor's name. The sudden silence was deathly. 'I know you'd never have arranged this,' Andrew said, 'if you'd known he's the leader who started all this. This isn't going to work for me.'

I got off the phone and asked God what to do. It was clear to me He'd gone to such extraordinary lengths to bring about a reconciliation, to rip open the double binds, to snap off the chains that were fettering Andrew, to jigsaw together a compromise where both parties were coming together on neutral ground, instead of one insisting that the other come to him in his own space.

I wanted to beat my head against the wall. 'Whoever gets a question in life, "What do you want?"' I asked God, 'and whoever thinks to herself, "Oh, yeah, what I really want is for a mantle that a friend of mine shouldn't have to be lifted off of him." If this is not Your moment of miracle, I don't know what is.'

'Why don't you ring Andrew back,' God suggested, 'and ask if he's willing to send his wife as his representative so she can get prayer on his behalf?'

'God, You are brilliant! Has anyone ever told You that?'

So that's what happened. The next day I met with the pastor and Andrew's wife—he was delighted but surprised to see her—and I outlined my understanding of the beginnings of Andrew's agoraphobia. As I explained about the mantle that needed removal, the pastor's face paled. It was clearly dawning on him that the church had created the problem in the first place. Then they'd made it far worse through a double bind. The mantle Andrew had been given was not only ill-fitting—like Saul's armour that David refused—it was dangerous. It was so overwhelming in its weight it had the power to incapacitate rather than protect.

The story ended well. The pastor prayed, the oppression on Andrew lifted that very day and he began baby-steps towards returning to work. But a decade of his life was in wreckage.

As I told Jenny about this long-ago series of events, I commented that I'd never thought I'd see a similar extreme level of godly coincidence in any situation ever again. It was a one-off in my view. It was so bizarre that I'd decided it was impossible for 'I can't pray for you' to recur. But since it had, and since I then recalled another incident where I'd been involved in a minor way interceding for a man whose leaders wouldn't pray for him during his separation, I grew suspicious. In that circumstance, which also involved deliverance, it turned out that the leaders were behind the separation.

So, as I spoke to Jenny about her own pastor refusing to initiate a deliverance session, my mind began to hard-ball all sorts of questions at me.

These situations were double binds. Did they have more in common than simply 'I can't pray for you'? Did they all involve mantles? Did the leadership emplace the double bind in, not just one case, but all of them?

There were other aspects that shrieked connection as well: deliverance, dishonour, isolation and, through it, silencing, soul violation and weaponisation of intercession. Furthermore, there was prolonged false loyalty to the leaders, as well as an inversion of responsibility by the leaders. Because the person seeking prayer could not fulfil a condition placed on them, the leaders felt absolved of any responsibility in the matter. They could project the blame away from themselves for the outcome and so ignore the abusive power structures they had built and were actively maintaining.

As my suspicions crystallised, I put a question to Jenny. 'Think back about two years or so. Is there a traumatic event involving the church and a mantle where your husband was dishonoured and silenced?'

Instantly she recalled such an event. Her husband had been invited to speak at their church and was looking forward to the opportunity. The topic was one very close to his heart. However, just before getting on stage, he'd been forbidden to talk on the very subject that was the passion and calling of his life. One of the pastors wanted to introduce that particular revelation to the church so, despite Jenny's husband's protest, he'd been prohibited from mentioning it. It had been such an unexpected, last-minute intervention, it had come as a traumatic shock.

Notice the connection between the initial ban and the later bind. 'Don't speak,' had been the first message. 'Because you can't speak,' came the later message, 'I can't pray for you.'

Now, although I've used 'double bind' in its ordinary sense throughout this discussion so far, the meaning actually overlaps with the understanding of 'binding' in the first century. Back then, 'binding' had two senses:

- first, tying a person up or putting them in fetters
- second, prohibiting a person from undertaking a certain action by invoking a legal authority

One was a physical sense; the other a spiritual one.

For the last century or so, deliverance ministry that involves a power encounter has been dominated by the technique of binding-and-silencing. Note what's happened here: a protocol that has been used to control demonic spirits has been extended in its use to constrain human spirits. Perhaps the words, 'I bind and silence you,' are not spoken aloud but the same thought is in operation. We can be sure that the origin of this thought is, in fact, in the arena of deliverance because of that unutterably strange secondary bind: 'I can't pray for you.' Just as the minister wouldn't pray for a demon, so now they won't pray for a human being. It's the same procedure.

God never removes freewill from us. Therefore anyone who double-binds us so there's no way out is not hearing from the Spirit of God, whether they think they are or not. It's terrifying to realise that those in leadership who act like this are not aware that love is gone. So is freedom. And so is that which sets us free—the truth. The Holy Spirit has left the building.

The refusal of the shepherd to go out and release the sheep that isn't lost but is trapped by the shepherd's own snares was unsettling. Surely, I thought, these would be rare scenarios.

But in the week that followed, other instances of double binds became apparent. As time went by, even more horrifying examples emerged. Not all of them emanated from church circles. Nevertheless, I'd become sensitised to the symptoms and hallmarks—the binding and silencing, the prohibitions, the dishonour, the isolation, the delays, the lack of responsibility, the theft of calling. I began to realise these were Catch-22 situations on steroids.[35]

- You're too traumatised to be able to do your job effectively. We admit to responsibility for the trauma. However, by delaying compensation to you for as long as possible, you won't have the money or emotional capacity to mount a legal case against us. We'll only pay up when you accept

the non-disclosure agreement you're currently refusing to sign.
- You've had a mastectomy because of cancer. You want your husband to sympathise with you about the loss of your breast but, when he does, you feel he doesn't want you without it. It's an emotional double bind.
- You need to pass a subject that is mandatory for a degree but you realise that, to do so, you'll need to compromise your integrity by agreeing with your lecturer's ideology. It's a double bind.
- You have questions about the unexplained discrepancies in the club's finances but you're repeatedly told you have trust issues. Your friend wants to be both president and treasurer of the club next year during the big convention. Your friend finally tells you she's spoken to her therapist and they've devised some rules of friendship you need to agree on from this point forward: you can't offer her help, you can't give her help, you can't ask her if she needs help, you can't check with others if she needs help, you can't ask anyone else to help her, you can't appoint anyone else to help her, you can't urge her to get help, you can't criticise her for not seeking help even if it's evident she needs it, you can't discuss this conversation about help with anyone—you are to support her by being always positive and never negative. If the big convention incurs a loss, you are to contribute to the shortfall without asking questions.

'So,' said the person being addressed in the last story, dissolving in tears, 'if you insist on this, it's the end of our friendship, you know that? Friends help each other in time of need. Do you really want me to be a friend by behaving as the opposite?'

'My therapist has said this is necessary.'

'No point in prolonging this, then. I resign from the club right now. And our friendship is over.'

There's a seemingly casual comment in that last story that comes up repeatedly in so many different cases—it's the attempt of the leader to wield control through ricocheting any problem back to the person raising it by stating: '*You* have trust issues.'

Maybe that's true. But the fact a sheep has trust issues does not confer trustworthiness on the shepherd.

After the deliverance minister finally remembered to turn up but then simply chatted during his brief visit, Jenny decided I was the right person to give prayer ministry to her husband. I had been praying for him but had resisted the idea of prayer ministry—prayer being entirely different in scope to prayer ministry—because I sensed he needed a power encounter with Jesus rather than a truth encounter.[36] In retrospect, that feeling was accurate. It wasn't until much later that I realised, in Scripture, there are several instances of leader-imposed double binds being overturned but *all* of them involve a power encounter. A truth encounter involves repentance and forgiveness and, although that was required in this situation, it wouldn't blast open the double bind.

As I was driving to meet up with Jenny and her husband, a single word kept drumming in my mind. The journey took a couple of hours and, during that time, one name kept obsessively pushing its way into my thoughts: 'Latipan... Latipan.'

I recognised the word as one I'd encountered several months previously. During my research into the Canaanite war goddess, Anat, I'd come across 'Latipan' as a title of her father, the elder-god, Bull El. It meant *shroudface*.

I was baffled. What did the name of a Canaanite deity have to do with the situation? Ok, sure, *shroudface* was a title that evoked death—but I intended to pray about that anyway. What was the significance of that specific word in the present circumstances? Why did I need to know 'Latipan' of all strange names? I just didn't understand why the Holy Spirit was so insistent on this word and not something simpler.

However, pressing in for understanding, it finally dawned on me that Canaanite '-pan' was similar to Hebrew 'paneh', *face*, while 'lati-' was obviously related to 'lot', *wrapping, covering* or *winding sheet*. But, on further consideration, that would mean 'lati-' was also linked to Lotan, the twisting, winding seven-headed serpent, the equivalent in Canaanite religion of the dragonish Leviathan.

Leviathan is a threshold spirit and throne guardian specialising in retaliation against dishonour. However, the primary presenting problem in the situation was a double bind. Certainly there was dishonour but it was exhibited by the leaders, not by the person trapped in the bind. Why was he copping the retaliation for dishonour that should have been featuring in the lives of the leaders instead? Of course, maybe it was present in their lives, but we just didn't know enough to spot it.

Still how did Leviathan factor into a double bind situation? It took me a long while to figure it out.

Double binds placed by leaders over those under their charge are, as I've mentioned, essentially the same as the binding-and-silencing technique used to control a demonic spirit. Leaders have moved on to controlling human spirits. They tie people up in the spiritual equivalent of winding sheets. These death *wrappings*, 'lotim', invoke Lotan—Leviathan the retaliator—over people's lives. Such shrouds have their origin in the occult. The word, 'lot', from 'lut', *wrap* or *envelop*, is related via consonance[37] to 'lat', *secrecy, mystery* or *incantation*. The Egyptian sorcerers, Jannes and Jambres,[38] used 'lat', *dark arts*, to reproduce the plague of blood and the plague of frogs, thereby allowing Pharaoh to harden his heart against God's spokesmen, Moses and Aaron, and their request to let the people go to worship God.

That's what we're looking at in these modern situations: a hardening of the heart by pharaoh-like leaders that results in others being denied access to God. Because of the double bind, it doesn't matter what decision any of us they've wrapped into a shroud make, we won't be able to escape dishonouring someone involved in the situation. It might be the leader who is dishonoured, it might be ourselves. Indirectly, God will be dishonoured because one of His beloved children, His unique creation, has been insulted and violated.

Now having called up Leviathan, the spirit-specialist in retaliation against dishonour, reprisal is inevitable. Violent payback is the natural consequence the leader has brought down into the lives of those under their charge through the emplacement of the double bind. Whether the leader is obeyed or not, the people are pulverised by the backlash from Leviathan's stinging, smashing tail. Their ability to enter their calling is either bound up in death wrappings or has been exploded and shattered without possibility of restoration.

But surely, you might think, that can't possibly be right. There must be a way out. There's simply got to be.

Did Jesus ever deal with such a problem? Yes, of course, He did. And in doing so, He reveals the hidden aspect of each one of these situations: every one of them involves *atonement*. There are several scenarios in Scripture involving double binds and atonement. Most involve violence, and not unnaturally result in further violence. In fact, one of these double-bind situations played a role in the decision to kill Jesus.

Every male over twenty years of age had to pay an annual tax of a half-shekel to the Temple. This requirement went back to the days of the Exodus and an ordinance concerning a census:

> *Then the Lord said to Moses, 'When you take a census of the Israelites to count them, each one must pay the Lord a ransom for his life at the time he is counted. Then no plague will come on them when you number them. Each one who crosses over to those already counted is to give a half shekel... This half shekel is an offering to the Lord. All who cross over, those twenty years old or more, are to give an offering to the Lord. The rich are not to give more than a half shekel and the poor are not to give less when you make the offering to the Lord to atone for your lives. Receive the atonement money from the Israelites and use it for the service of the tent of meeting. It will be a memorial for the Israelites before the Lord, making atonement for your lives.'*

> Exodus 30:11–16 NIV

Now, in the early first century, the Sanhedrin under Annas had created a double bind in relation to this atonement tax. It came about because the Roman overlords of Judea did not allow the ruling council to strike their own coins. There were many different currencies in circulation but the chief priests decided that, for the Temple tax, only a special half-shekel would be deemed to be a legitimate payment. They therefore had to order these coins from a foreign mint. There were quite a few production houses to choose from across the ancient world—and, naturally, the different mints varied in the quality of the finish they offered, as well as the quantity of silver in the coin. They also varied in their willingness to supply bespoke designs.

The chief priests decided the sterling content of the coin was more important than the design motif, so they chose the half-shekels from the mint at Tyre—a production house that did not offer any customisation. The Tyrian shekel had, on one side, an image of Herakles-Melqart, a combination of Hercules, the superhuman strong man of legend, and Melqart, the king of the city of death. On the reverse were engraved the words, 'Tyre Holy and Inviolable.'

So here's the double bind: if a person paid the tax, he blasphemed by offering to God a graven image as an atonement sacrifice.[39] Instead of a memorial placed before the Lord to honour Him and display covenant loyalty, a blasphemous image would remain there to insult Him. Alternatively, if the person didn't pay the atonement tax, he laid himself open to plague for disobeying a specific command of God. Plague was specifically mentioned as a consequence of refusing to pay the appointed ransom.

To pay or not to pay? That was the question. Either way, God was dishonoured and consequently retaliation, as meted out by Leviathan, the spirit of backlash, was inevitable. To make the set-up still worse, Annas and his family had a sophisticated rort going. Since these coins were not in ordinary circulation, people had to buy them. The exchange rate was exorbitant. Annas had paid the Romans to be appointed to the high priesthood and, although the position should have been for life, he was deposed after about ten years. However he was followed—though not immediately—by his son-in-law Caiaphas and was thus able to continue his money-making racket. Four of Annas' sons and a grandson followed Caiaphas into the office of high priest.

The family had a stranglehold on the position and they used it to enrich themselves. They operated four booths on the Mount of Olives, specialising in the sale of sacrificial offerings. In addition, in the month before the Passover, money-changers were stationed in the 'bazaars of the sons of Annas' in the Temple courtyard to facilitate the collection of the Temple tax. They traded ordinary currency for the special half-shekel at an outrageous mark-up.

Most scholars, in commenting on this episode in the gospels, focus on the injustice and the price-gouging that so disadvantaged the poor. But this spiritual abuse was far more insidious than mere crooked money-making.

It was not just a national disgrace, not just exploitation of the poor, not just corruption in the sanctuary, not just contempt of the holy, not just the utmost sacrilege, not just denial of the atonement that enabled drawing near to God, it was the perpetration of a vile and unspeakable bind involving Melqart, the death-lord, who was the equivalent of Moloch—an idol appeased by human sacrifice. By invoking Moloch, and allowing him a presence in the Temple, the chief priests were trussing the people up in death wrappings.

In compelling the Jews to make *an atonement offering* by trading with coins that had an image of Melqart on them, they were forcing the people into covenant with Moloch. Or alternatively, if the people chose to refuse to pay, then they were forcing them into a breach of covenant with God. Dubbing the Pharisees who were in agreement with the actions of the high priest as *'you brood of vipers,'*[40] is really very mild, when you think about the situation: the leaders were conspiring to force people into sin.

The chief priests had allowed the city-god of Tyre into the Temple—the very same rebel angel Ezekiel had once revealed to have been a guardian cherub in the mountain of God. Like the cherubim who watched over the mercy seat, where the blood of atonement was sprinkled, the spirit-king of Tyre similarly overshadowed and covered. But instead of guarding the blood, in which was the life and the price of ransom, he traded with it. He trafficked in names[41]—and thus with all that God has attached to names: reputations, destinies and callings, lives and rights, blessings and inheritances. His commercialisation of the atonement was so abhorrent, he was cast out of God's presence for trading.

> *You were the signet of perfection, full of wisdom and perfect in beauty. You were in Eden, the garden of God... You were an anointed guardian cherub. I placed you; you were on the holy mountain of God; in the midst of the stones of fire you walked... In the abundance of your trade you were filled with violence in your midst, and you sinned; so I cast you as a profane thing from the mountain of God.*
>
> Ezekiel 28:13-16 ESV

Annas and Caiaphas had not just welcomed the image of the spirit-king of Tyre into the earthly Temple via the coinage they chose, they had also embraced his obsession with trading and with desecration of the atonement.

Jesus was incensed at every aspect of this defilement. So He took action—not verbal action, but forceful physical action. It was clear words weren't enough. As God had once cast the guardian cherub out of His garden and mountain, and therefore out of the heavenly Temple, so now Jesus prepared to cast out

Herakles-Melqart, the strongman death-lord, from the earthly Temple.

It was not, in fact, His office to do so, even though it had been prophesied that He would take this role. He did so because others had abandoned their appointed responsibilities. Leviathan, as mentioned previously in this series,[42] was originally a highly-placed courtier of God assigned the duty of maintaining and enforcing honour within the heavenly sanctuary. The counterpart of Leviathan within the earthly Temple was the Levite priesthood. It was their task to ensure that the Temple and environs were holy and set apart from the profane. It was their role to guard the consecration of the sanctuary as a place of prayer and sacred reverence, to protect it as a space where worshippers could draw near to God.

The Levites had effectively deserted their posts. So had the chief priests and the ruling council. And the high priest wasn't about to release the nation from the double bind he had imposed.

Now I don't doubt if there was any other alternative than plaiting a whip—this indicates the intentionality of His action, its lack of spontaneity—and moving around the Temple courtyard to take out the money-changers, along with the sellers of sacrificial birds and livestock, Jesus would have taken it. He wouldn't have wanted to parallel the violence that the spirit-king of Tyre had specialised in with his trafficking. So clearly there was no longer any other way to enforce honour except to be like Leviathan—to wield the stinging, lashing tail that chases away, out of God's presence, any creature who lacks respect for Him or any part of His creation.

Long ago, it had been prophesied that the Messiah would come as a seraph. At least that was the traditional rabbinic interpretation of Isaiah's warning to the Philistines on the death of King Ahaz:

> *Do not rejoice, all you Philistines, that the rod that struck you is broken. For a viper will spring from the root of the snake, and a flying serpent from its egg.*

Isaiah 14:29 BSB

The Hebrew word translated *viper* here in this passage is 'nachash', while *flying serpent* is 'seraph', the same as the six-winged angels who called to each other, 'Holy, holy, holy,' in Isaiah's vision of the throneroom of God. The word 'nachash' is elsewhere used by Isaiah to describe Leviathan[43] where it is translated *serpent*. The Jewish sages saw Isaiah's words against the Philistines as awaiting fulfilment by the Messiah.

In using words he otherwise connected with Leviathan, Isaiah prophesied retaliation against Greek colonial settlers, for that was what the Philistine invaders were. And in Jesus' attack against

Herakles-Melqart, there is precisely the Greek-strongman component we should expect for the realisation of this prophecy.

So, here we have the Lord's own solution to the issue of a double bind that involves the atonement: ask Jesus to bring a whip to the situation.

Every set of circumstances that centres around a mantle or a calling—that is, a legacy or an inheritance—also involves some aspect of atonement. Our callings, our destinies, our inheritances have to be ransomed from the power of the enemy. Jesus has already accomplished this for us through His atonement on the Cross. But access to His great work is compromised by leaders who try to trade mantles—or sometimes even collect them—by misusing their authority to place us in double binds. This is entirely contrary to their own vocation as leaders in the priesthood of all believers—just as the Levites were called to intercede with God for the people and open up the way of atonement, so today's leaders are called to partner with Jesus in introducing believers ever more deeply into the benefits of His atonement. Instead, some are doing the opposite. Through the double binds they impose, our ability to receive the finished work of Christ's atonement is compromised.

Once we've been set up so that there's no way we can *not* dishonour, inevitably we're going to score a round of retaliation whatever we do. Jesus Himself did so. His intervention in the Temple threatened the extortion racket Annas and Caiaphas had going—they, after all, were the authorities that the money-changers represented. This action by Jesus was the decisive one in bringing about His death.

Inevitably also, some leaders are going to justify putting the double bind in place because of the anger and dishonour we exhibit while struggling to free ourselves of the constraints. These leaders retrospectively rationalise their actions in the face of our reaction, or as a result of the outcome.

Jenny's husband eventually died—allegedly, according to some leaders who'd formerly proclaimed themselves his friends, because he didn't have enough faith for healing. But they were amongst the ones who didn't pray for him, and who had maintained, 'I can't pray for you.'

Now quite apart from the fact it's the faith of Jesus that saves—our own mustard-seed's worth being effective only when it's united to His—where was *their* faith? Sometimes, as we see in the account of the four detectives[44] who lowered a paralysed man down through a roof in order to lay him at Jesus' feet, it's about the faith of our friends, not that of the individual. The daughter of Jairus had no faith—she was probably too sick to even be aware her father had gone to seek Jesus. It's also unlikely the servant of the centurion stationed at Capernaum had faith since he probably didn't know that his master intended to ask Jesus for help. Both the girl and the servant were healed because someone petitioned Jesus on their behalf.

So any suggestion that a sick person doesn't have enough faith for healing reeks of irresponsibility and self-justification. If we haven't done our part—as the centurion, or the four friends, or Jairus—then this is a hypocritical statement. Yet it's an attitude so many of us face today when leaders place double binds over our lives, then refuse to remove them, and even double down on tightening them still further. Moreover, just as Jesus did, we inevitably face retaliation and death threats—if not physical death, then death of reputation, death of career and death of relationship.

'Don't talk about this. Anyone who talks about this is under a curse. Don't you know that your leaders have the ability to curse you?'

Jenny (a third Jenny) was explaining the latest developments in the ongoing saga of crisis in her church. A guest speaker had come in and warned the congregation not to gossip about the founder who had been credibly accused of multiple instances of sexual and financial abuse. A direction not to gossip is fine. An implied threat is not. I said to Jenny that cursing is never okay.

'Maybe he didn't say exactly that about cursing us. I'd need to check,' Jenny said.

No, you don't need to check, I thought. Even if he didn't say precisely those words, even if he can plausibly deny there was any intention of threat, that was obviously how the words came across. *Besides*, I thought to myself, *I've been through the steps of this dance routine on several occasions now. I'm starting to recognise it. This particular pirouette is called 'false loyalty'.*

'Cursing is never ok,' I told her. 'Whatever happened to "Love your enemies; do good to those who hate you"?'

The exercise of authority by church leaders has, all too often, become an issue of damage control. Rather than bring truth and transparency into play, this misuse of authority was an overt attempt at domination and manipulation. Authority was no longer being used with rightful and righteous intent—to uphold the Word of God, as is its design—but about ensuring the leadership could hold on to power.

Quite some time later, I realised that the peculiar question, 'Don't you know that your leaders have the ability to curse you?' emanates out of *Covering Theology*.[45] Both blessing and cursing are tied up with Covering Theology and so engender a great deal of anxiety. There can be fear of missing out on a blessing or alternatively a fear of losing protection and being cursed for choosing to disobey a leader's directive and thus defying their authority. But this is to misunderstand authority. Any believer, irrespective of whether they are a leader or not, who speaks of cursing another has already lost authority. That's because authority is given to uphold the word and the will of God, not to pick and choose which Scriptures are convenient and useful for us and thus to exercise power on our own behalf.

Such words are not about modelling the great and first commandment—*love God*—along with its like-patterned corollary—*love your neighbour as yourself,* but about retaining ascendancy over others for the benefit of those at the top of the hierarchy. And because the words are outside of God's expressed will, they indicate the leaders have stepped outside of the chain of authority that goes back to the Lord Himself.

They may still hold leadership positions but their authority has become corrupt. They are exercising power on their own behalf, not bowing to God Most High.

A very similar double bind to the one the chief priests created in the time of Jesus came about when absolute power got the better of David. He decided he needed to know how many troops he could muster in time of war, so he ordered a census of the fighting men. Joab, the head of David's army, along with his sub-commanders approached David to ask him to rescind the directive. Now, 1 Chronicles 21:1 says that it was the satan who incited David to take this census. 2 Samuel 24:1, on the other hand, says it was God who incited David to do so. The two accounts are not mutually exclusive nor necessarily contradictory.

As the first chapter of the Book of Job recounts, the satan appeared before God to ask permission to test Job. God grants this, but ultimately takes responsibility for the outcome by later saying that the satan incited Him against Job. (Job 2:3)

Thus it would appear from the two different accounts regarding David's census that the satan incited David to count the fighting men because God gave permission for him to test David. This does not absolve David of surrendering to the satan's pressure and therefore failing the test of trusting in God for the protection of the nation.

David didn't listen to Joab and insisted the census go ahead. Nearly ten months went by and, in all that time, David didn't realise he was defying God. A census was not forbidden, but an atonement tax had to be paid in order to avoid a plague breaking out.[46] It seems that, in those ten months, David's daily meditation on the Torah—required of him as king—didn't manage to reach the thirtieth chapter of Exodus.

Now this atonement tax is the same as that used by Annas and Caiaphas to create a double bind. David created a similar double bind by demanding a census but choosing to ignore God's requirement for a ransom to be paid.

Joab was so revolted by David's order he didn't count the Levites or the tribe of Benjamin. (Since he had a blood feud with one of the clans of Benjamin, but apparently protected them anyway, the depth of his revulsion is apparent.)[47] Finally it dawned on David that he'd sinned. He was conscience-stricken. At that point, he was given three options by God: three years of famine, three months of pursuit by enemies or three days of plague. David chooses to fall into the hands of the Lord and, with that selection, seventy thousand people died from plague.

Those under his care, the people of Israel he'd supposedly been shepherding, pay the price. That's the usual outcome when leaders demand unquestioning obedience and unhesitating submission. In doing so, they insist on the level of loyalty and trust that should be given only to God. Once again, a leader denied access to the atonement by creating a double bind and demanding his own way, regardless.

The third Jenny alerted me to another instance of a double bind. Did it involve a mantle? I might have thought otherwise, had not Jenny Two told me what transpired at her husband's deathbed. A pastor from her church finally came to the hospital but again, instead of praying, had simply waited for hours in hopes of receiving her husband's mantle. After this ghoulish experience, Jenny Two became conscious of the passing of a legacy from one generation to the next. She came across a story about a well-known pastor that she found unsettling. This pastor had gone to the deathbed of a prominent minister and asked for her mantle to be imparted to him.

Maybe this was ok, maybe not. However, any passing of spiritual inheritance involves the atonement. Subsequently, the pastor organised an event and, during it, some women leaders prayed about sexual abuse. One exhorted, 'Repent for your offenders because it was a spirit after us and not them.'

Now you can forgive offenders but you can't repent for them. Repentance is a work in the offender's life that, in partnership with Jesus, needs to be negotiated in fear and trembling. To conflate victim and offender is to suggest the one wounded is as guilty of sin as the wrongdoer. It's gas-lighting, as well as a betrayal of innocence. Furthermore while it's true the spirit of abuse is indeed after us, that does not at any point negate the complicity of the perpetrator with the spirit. Threshold spirits tempt, but they cannot compel. It may seem like they can at times, but that's because we've chosen to be seduced so often by them that we've come to crave the fix and the release. The prayer as it stands is perilously close to excusing any criminal endeavour and to judging the victim as liable for the offence. To project the responsibility for evil choices back to the victims is to double bind them into the role of both perpetrator and victim.

During the same event, another speaker reinforced this thoughtless exhortation with this declaration. 'We renounce trauma. We will not dwell on our trauma or continue to talk about our trauma. We judge the altars of trauma and bitterness in our own soul.'

All altars involve trauma. Every last one of them. That's because all altars involve sacrifice. And the ultimate altar—the place of the all-sufficient sacrifice—is the Cross of Jesus. Maybe the speaker didn't mean to renounce the Cross along with the atonement of the Lord but that, in the fine legal niceties with which the demonic excels, is precisely what happened. This is not hair-splitting; it's precisely the ambiguity of language that spirits like Python use to trap us into double binds. To follow Christ by renouncing the Cross of Christ is a perversion.

To renounce any talk about trauma is not a way to resolve it but rather to lock it in place for generations. Mark Wolyn[48] speaks of the descendants of Holocaust survivors who know exactly what horrors their parents or grandparents experienced despite never hearing a word about what happened. The epigenetic impact of the trauma can only be put to rights by dealing with the memory and bringing it to the Light, not by deciding not to dwell or talk about it and thus forget it, or by condemning it as rooted in bitterness. The Living Water is the healer; judgment never is.

There have been times when I've felt it necessary to counsel people: 'There's only one thing you did wrong and it's not what you were told. And it's not what you were accused of, either. You should not have repented. So now you need to repent of your repentance.'

Often that initial—and inappropriate—repentance has been the result of pressure by a leader. People are coerced into agreeing to refrain from speaking out. They're silenced; their calling is shut down; their warnings are quenched; their counsel is muzzled. They're asked to trust that the leaders will protect others from harm by the abuser but also never to question the process the leaders choose. They are asked to forgo due diligence and to offer the leaders the kind of trust that should only ever be given to God. If they've suffered trauma, they are often re-traumatised by their own sidelining as they witness the care and compassion offered to the offender that is denied to the victim.

A significant number of leaders today have returned to the philosophy of the Pharisees—that wealth and power are signs of the blessing and favour of God. The more money you have and the more prestige attached to your name, then the more righteous you are in God's eyes—that's the way many first century Jews thought. That's why the disciples of Jesus were so astonished when He announced it was almost impossible for a rich man to enter the Kingdom of God. *What hope is there*, they thought, *for the rest of us?*

Now, we know better than to think like this. Or do we? Maybe it's not about wealth or power, but is it about our status because of the gifts God has given us? Do the gifts cause us to be blind to our own unrighteousness? And consequently blind to our favourite faith heroes? So, when the faults and flaws of Elijah and Elisha, Moses and Abraham, Joseph and Noah, Samuel and David (I truly cannot help laughing at those who try to deny David breached the Torah's prohibition on a king marrying many wives by suggesting 18 wives is not *that* many) are exposed to the light when Jesus sets to work mending them, are we like the disciples? Do we think: *what hope is there for the rest of us?*

Today, when a church is flourishing and the leadership team expanding, there's a tendency to back-formulate from 'God is blessing us' to 'His favour means we're both right and righteous.' David did exactly this when he wrote his own eulogy. He essentially said that he must have been a good guy because God approved of him, as evidenced through His gift of a covenant. But David's reasoning assumes that God's grace is only offered to the deserving, not to the underserving. This is not just a misunderstanding but a misrepresentation.

Instead of recognising that the gifts and offices of God are irrevocable, we are like David and tend towards the judgment that no leader could be in sin and still operate with an obviously powerful authority or anointing. This is a fatal assumption. God does not remove gifts because of an unholy lifestyle—they wouldn't be *gifts* if He did. We are called to be spiritually discerning by examining the fruit of people's lives, not the gifts they are exercising.

Paul points out, in advocating a 'more excellent way' than pursuing gifts like healing, miracles, tongues, interpretation or administrative helps, that love is greater than them all—even greater than faith and hope.[49] It's easy to understand why as we look around so many churches today. Without love, the gifts are weaponised against other members of the Body. Without love, as we've seen in so many of the stories in this book, faith is a weapon—a missile of accusation rather than a shower of blessing.

Now, of course, if anyone actually does suspect rampant, repeated, unrepented sin in a leader's life and has the courage to bring it to the attention of anyone involved in the oversight of the church then, more often than not, binding-and-silencing kicks in as does the weaponisation of Scripture: *'Touch not Mine anointed.'*[50]

The Hebrew word for *touch* is the same as that for *plague* and *striking with physical force*. It's about both violence and the curse of covenant violation. This verse is therefore not a ban on exposing corrupt behaviour; it's a sanction against bodily aggression as well as speaking out maledictions and calling down evil on the head of the offender. Instead of cursing, blessing is called for.

> *Bless those who persecute you; bless and do not curse.*
>
> Romans 12:14 NKJV

But this works both ways, for both leaders and followers. The guest speaker who said something along the lines of, 'Don't you know that your leaders have the ability to curse you?' was so far out of line, it's tragic. I'm always reminded, when I hear, or hear of, someone saying, 'I'm anointed and appointed,' that so was the bejewelled rebel angel who walked amongst the fiery stones on the mountain of God.

Apart from the weaponisation of Scripture, the other common binding-and-silencing routine goes like this: 'You must keep quiet about this for the sake of the gospel.' As if the gospel is served by cover-up and deceit. By allowing a leader to keep sin hidden and unrepented, we create a space of allurement. Abusers are attracted to the spiritual dynamic in that space because there they can indulge their vices without being exposed. Ultimately, by remaining 'silent for the sake of the gospel' then, instead of nipping any issues in the bud or early in their flowering, we allow them to ripen to their full toxic potential before their destructive power is unleashed.

Leaders who fear the shame of having their sin exposed often do not fear the shame of committing the sin in the first place. It's unfortunate the actual shame of exposure is often the only thing keeping them from repetition: it's not repentance, it's not the pain they've inflicted on others, it's not the destruction they've wreaked on relationships. Their fear of shame or their desire for power—or both—leads them into complicity with the fallen threshold spirits; the powers that are working so hard to block us from passing over into our calling. The threshold spirits particularly target leaders because they are the ones with the authority to create double binds in the lives of others and so deny us full access to the atonement. People who do not have authority over us don't have the power to build the bind—we simply shrug at them and ignore them.

Now although I've used the term 'leader' throughout this discussion, note that it would always be more accurate to say 'the one who has power over us.' So, by 'leader', I don't necessarily mean the one in authority. Consider it instead, from here on out, to be a shorthand way of saying 'the one to whom we have granted power over ourselves'. Generally speaking, this will indeed be the person in immediate positional authority over us but, in certain situations, it may not be. For example, the Gibeonites were despised and marginalised servants within the society of ancient Israel. But, as we'll see, David ceded power to them by asking them what they wanted to bless the land.

From that moment on, the slaves had power over the king. They were the 'leaders' thereafter and they didn't just create one horrific double bind, they multiplied them one on top of the other.

Many fine leaders today are in fact in difficulties, stress and burnout, at least in part because they've given other people power over them—they've made the kind of surrender that should only ever be handed to God. A place of extreme stress or anxiety is not a place for wise decision-making—it is a transition space for choosing to turn *to* God or *from* Him, for deepening faith radically or for a collapse into unfaith. It's in these circumstances of uncertainty and worry that the spirit of wasting tempts otherwise godly pastors to solve at least a few of their issues with the first wrapping of what will become a double bind.

People trapped by double binds tend to lose their faith in the 'church', if not God. There are hints that precisely this happened to David—he became afraid to go to the Tabernacle.

When we've been knotted into a double bind by a leader influenced by a cabal of ungodly threshold spirits, then we're locked into a position where, whatever we do, we're unable to fling off the death wrappings, unable to reach for the atonement, unable to benefit from the salvation Jesus has won for us. It's that serious. That's why we need to invite Jesus into the situation and ask Him to brandish a whip as He cleans it out.

Because this is an attempt by the threshold spirits to strip us of salvation. They're no longer satisfied with an agenda to disinherit us and rob us of our calling, it's become about shredding our salvation and taking down as many aspects of it as possible. Salvation, after all, includes not just a berth in heaven, but rescue in the here-and-now. It's not merely future-oriented but also involves redeeming the past and sanctifying the present with restoration and ransom, health and wholeness, justice and recompense, peace and inheritance.

Anyone who double binds us and thus compromises our entry into the fullness of such salvation has to have a huge question mark over their own salvation. It's as if they don't want to see anyone gain what they themselves have turned their back on. That might seem a harsh judgmental statement, but I believe there's precedent for it in the most unusual parable Jesus ever told.

Salvation is all about the atonement of Jesus. Nothing else. *Nothing*.

Nothing we do, not even forgiveness or repentance, can—in its own right—have even the slightest effect on our salvation. Forgiveness is only effective when it's empowered by the atonement of Jesus. Repentance only results in lasting change when it's given activated life through the atonement of Jesus.

Nothing in heaven or on earth can withstand the atoning power of the blood of Jesus.

And because nothing can, we are apt to become complacent. We all too often think that the diabolic powers who oppose the Most High God will just stand aside when we invoke its efficacy on our behalf. It's true that sometimes they do—just to seduce us into thinking they always will.

It doesn't occur to us, unfortunately, that they'd search and research until they found a way, not to overcome the atonement—since that's impossible—but to circumvent it and so render its covenantal protection ineffective. Even though there's precedent for exactly that.

When the Israelites were on the verge of entering the Promised Land, the king of Moab became alarmed by their presence. He employed the diviner Balaam to curse them from the heights above their encampment. Three times, however, Balaam blessed the nation of Israel. Finally, to save his head and get his pay, Balaam offered the king a strategy, a workaround, to negate God's defensive canopy over the people.

Balaam's thinking followed these lines: *God will never fail to keep His covenant. It's therefore necessary to tempt the Israelites into violating the covenant themselves and thus losing its umbrella of protection. An easy way to achieve this would be to send to their camp some beautiful priestesses of Baal-Peor to seduce the men into ritual sex. Through this cultic activity they'll become 'one with the god', as they will when they participate in a feast offered to Baal-Peor.*

It's being 'at one' that defines the act of *atone*ment. Ultimately all rebel threshold spirits are busy, trying to deactivate the atoning power of the blood of Jesus in our lives. They're not omnipotent or omniscient, so they can't focus their attention on us all the time—only when we become a sustained threat as we begin to work out our salvation in fear and trembling and start to apply the atonement to ever-wider and deeper parts of our hearts.

The fact that, through simple testing of our faith, they achieve so much of their agenda shows the depth of our complicity with them and just what a hold they have in our lives. Their control over our thinking is so strong we interpret trials as attacks and, misguidedly, often try to bind and silence them. In doing so, we step outside our authority. We do not have the right to operate contrary to the Word of God and, if we do, we hand to these spirits further judicial rights to challenge us.

The closer Jesus draws us to Himself and the closer we draw to Jesus, the more we will jettison the impediments in our lives that give the enemy a legal foothold to bar us from our inheritance in Him. And so, the greater threat we become.

Now it's hard enough to believe in the atonement without the active hostility of these fallen threshold guardians. In fact, it's impossible. In far too many instances we are our own worst enemy—we personally create our own double binds to prevent ourselves moving beyond any boundary that feels unsafe or that seems unbearably risky. We put these double binds in place when we reach the limit of our trust in God. But these double binds are quite different from the ones created by leaders—they are internal; they're under our control, not outside it; they're made so that we feel secure once we are on the verge of a perilously high-risk zone. They are not like the external double binds, placed over us without our consent and which are designed to deprive us of some aspect of salvation—perhaps calling, perhaps health, perhaps recompense, perhaps inheritance. Internal double binds are put in place so we feel safe, even if we are not; external double binds place us in danger, even if they are alleged to be for our protection. No double bind—internal or external—is good, but the externally imposed ones are almost always traumatic and thus devastatingly destructive to the soul.

We get so focussed on the external double bind and how to escape it, we lose our focus on the Lord. Our unbelief in the atonement, always a problem anyway, becomes insurmountable.

Jesus told a parable about a rich man and a beggar named Lazarus. It's the only story He ever told where one of the characters has a name.

There was a certain rich man who was splendidly clothed in purple and fine linen and who lived each day in luxury. At his gate lay a poor man named Lazarus who was covered with sores. As Lazarus lay there longing for scraps from the rich man's table, the dogs would come and lick his open sores.

Finally, the poor man died and was carried by the angels to sit beside Abraham at the heavenly banquet. The rich man also died and was buried, and he went to the place of the dead. There, in torment, he saw Abraham in the far distance with Lazarus at his side.

The rich man shouted, 'Father Abraham, have some pity! Send Lazarus over here to dip the tip of his finger in water and cool my tongue. I am in anguish in these flames.'

But Abraham said to him, 'Son, remember that during your lifetime you had everything you wanted, and Lazarus had nothing. So now he is here being comforted, and you are in anguish. And besides, there is a great chasm separating us. No one can cross over to you from here, and no one can cross over to us from there.'

Then the rich man said, 'Please, Father Abraham, at least send him to my father's home. For I have five brothers, and I want him to warn them so they don't end up in this place of torment.'

> *But Abraham said, 'Moses and the prophets have warned them. Your brothers can read what they wrote.'*
>
> *The rich man replied, 'No, Father Abraham! But if someone is sent to them from the dead, then they will repent of their sins and turn to God.'*
>
> *But Abraham said, 'If they won't listen to Moses and the prophets, they won't be persuaded even if someone rises from the dead.'*

Luke 16:19–31 NLT

Who is the rich man dressed in purple? We learn he has five brothers and, although he has the Law of Moses, it has meant nothing to him during his lifetime. Jesus points out that, even if someone named Lazarus were to rise from the dead, it would make no difference to those who have turned their backs on the commandments given through Moses—those rules that Rabbi Hillel had summarised for a prospective Gentile convert who'd asked to be taught the Torah while standing on one foot: 'Whatever you find hateful, do not do to your neighbour—this is the whole of the Law, all the rest is commentary. Go and learn it.'

Jesus had a similar summary: love God and love your neighbour.

His parable is very pointed. Those who originally heard it would have had no doubts about the identity of the rich man. There weren't too many men who wore purple and had five brothers—strictly brothers-in-law in our own era, but not back in the first century when 'brothers' and 'brothers-in-law' were the same word—and who wouldn't believe even when Lazarus rose from the dead.

It was Caiaphas.

Only Luke tells this story of Jesus warning the high priest he's heading for Hades and hellfire. Indeed, Luke may have included it as a caution to one of the five brothers-in-law—'most excellent' Theophilus, the addressee of the third gospel. The title 'most excellent' is one that would have been used for the high priest, so there is a reasonable probability that Theophilus, who was the high priest from 38–42 AD, commissioned Luke's investigation.

The raising of Lazarus from the dead happened in real life. Whether the parable was told as a prophecy of what was to come—both the miraculous return from the grave and the reaction of the chief priests who, as a consequence, wanted to murder both Jesus and Lazarus—or whether it was told after the event, Caiaphas did not alter his behaviour.

It is no coincidence that, when Simon declares Jesus to be the Messiah, he is given the name 'Cephas'. This is basically the same as Caiaphas, indicating that Caiaphas' calling in life was to be the first to announce the Messiah to the public. It is also no coincidence that Simon is renamed Cephas on the Day of Atonement, Yom Kippur. Although we usually translate Cephas as *rock*, it is more accurately *cornerstone*, the very first building block to be laid for a new dwelling. The cornerstone was under the doorway where it would catch the blood dripping down from lintel and doorposts during a threshold covenant. Because it was a covenant, it naturally involved atonement, at_one_ment, a unity of hearts and minds concerning hospitality and defence. Thus Caiaphas' name was indicative in itself of atonement and, in creating a double bind for the nation over the atonement, he was deforming the identity and destiny that was prophesied within his own name. He'd placed what later Irish writers would call a 'geas' over himself. No wonder Jesus warned him of the consequences of the abuse he was perpetrating.

The story of Lazarus also features bindings and death wrappings. At the finale of the story, when Lazarus has come out of the tomb, still tied up in strips of linen with a shroud over his face, Jesus says:

> *'Unbind him and let him go.'*
>
> John 11:44 NASB

The word for *unbind* is precisely the same as *loose*, found in the 'binding and loosing' expressions that are the background of so much spiritual warfare today. The phrase 'binding and loosing' was common in Jesus' day. Back then *binding* had a physical meaning, a legislative meaning and an occult meaning.

It's to those original senses that we turn in the next chapter.

Prayer

Please remember to use the prayers throughout this book as a starting point for a conversation with God, not as a formula.

Father in heaven,

I believe that the power of the atonement of Jesus of Nazareth is all-sufficient, all-SUFFICIENT, ALL-sufficient. Help my unbelief.

I believe that the power of the atonement of Jesus is sufficient to overcome even denial of access to itself and to every lockout that would deprive me of the blessings of His atonement. Help my unbelief.

I believe that the power of the atonement of Jesus is sufficient to remove every one of the double binds inspired by the enemy of my soul and spoken over my life by those in authority over me. Help my unbelief.

I believe that the power of the atonement of Jesus is sufficient to unwind and unbind the death wrappings I have been encased in by the double binds. Help my unbelief.

I believe that the power of the atonement of Jesus is sufficient to negate the death threats against my reputation, my position, my job, my giftings and my calling. Help my unbelief.

I believe that the power of the atonement of Jesus is sufficient to dismantle my unmantling and to restore the mantle Jesus has given me as my inheritance. Help my unbelief.

I believe that the power of the atonement of Jesus is sufficient to heal the trauma of betrayal and of being strapped into a double bind by someone I looked up to and trusted. Help my unbelief.

I believe that the power of the atonement of Jesus of Nazareth is all-sufficient, all-SUFFICIENT, ALL-sufficient. Help my unbelief.

I ask that Jesus through the power of His atonement activate the declarations I have just made, granting them vigorous growth, solid maturity and abundant fruit so that my renewed and restored walk of faith is one that draws others to Him.

Thank You, Father, in the name of Jesus of Nazareth,

                                                Amen.

5

Binding

'As long as a man has an object under consideration, he is not one with it.' In fact what he has done is to estrange himself from the person or thing.

Charles Ringma
quoting Meister Eckhardt
Hear the Ancient Wisdom

ONE OF THE MOST COMMON PRACTICES in spiritual warfare and protective prayer is the custom of binding and silencing a demonic spirit.

I personally do not believe this has biblical warrant. Let me be upfront in saying I've always felt uncomfortable about it. But I never questioned it because it seemed no one else had any qualms. Still I refrained from participating and, on the one or two occasions I unthinkingly said, 'Amen,' in response to a leader's declaration, I felt immediate conviction.[51] I believe, in retrospect, that the sense of having done something wrong was a warning from the Holy Spirit.

Since bringing my unease out into the open, I've realised I'm far from the only person who feels disquiet when it comes to binding. I've also realised how contentious an issue it swiftly becomes, once it's raised publicly.

So let's try to marshal the facts and see if we can tiptoe safely through the minefield.

- Jesus did not ever bind an unclean spirit. He rebuked them, He cast them out, but there is not a single recorded instance of a binding on His part.
- Jesus did not bind any high-ranking ungodly spirits either. He did not bind the devil during His temptation in the wilderness and, when He contended with other so-called gods, He conducted His battles by repeatedly proving He was the legitimate owner of the names and titles they claimed the rights to. There is no mention that He ever bound them. (See, for example, John 6:19 where Jesus is seen walking on the water,[52] thereby demonstrating that Asherah is not entitled to be called 'She Who Walks On Water'.)
- There is no witness in the gospels or epistles to any of the apostles binding an unclean or demonic spirit or an angelic majesty. Paul cast the spirit of Python out of a girl, but no mention of binding is made.[53]
- We are specifically told that, in any confrontation with angelic majesties—that is, high level fallen spirits—any declaration other than, 'The Lord

- rebuke you,' is an arrogant rejection of authority that brings defilement to our bodies and has dire and potentially fatal consequences. (See: Jude 1:8–11 and 2 Peter 2:10–16.)
- We are specifically told how unwise it is to try to catch and bind Leviathan and that, if we happen to lay a hand on it, we will always remember the battle and never do it again. (See: Job 41:1–10.)
- Jesus used the terminology 'binding and loosing' when He announced the formation of His church, the 'ekklesia'. The phrase was a common formula in rabbinic legislation of the time and referred to judicial rulings relating to matters that were not specifically covered by the Torah. *Binding* referred to a proclamation prohibiting a particular activity, while *loosing* referred to permitting it.
- When used in reference to spirits during the first century, *binding* commonly denoted spells and incantations performed during occult rituals for the purpose of commanding the unswerving obedience of the spirits.[54] Both blessings and curses were invoked. Such spellbinding was designed to dominate others—whether those others were godlings, goddesses, angels, elemental beings or members of humanity—and to deny their freewill choices in order that the desire of the magic practitioner was carried out.

The absence of any reference to the binding of a spirit by Jesus or His disciples should give us pause. Serious pause. The silence of the gospels is not approval. In fact, taking into account the first century context of occult binding by exorcists and practitioners of magic, the silence more likely points to quiet criticism. When we further factor in the cautions of Jude and Peter telling us to restrict ourselves to asking the Lord to rebuke the higher level spirits, our serious pause should lengthen.

But, so many people will protest, we have been given *all authority* by Jesus. That means, so it's said, we are not limited by the injunctions about Leviathan or the warnings given to us by the apostles.

This is a complete and fundamental misunderstanding of the nature of authority. To think that 'all authority' means that we have been given the power to ignore the Word of God is to act like a rogue judge who disdains the law and flouts it whenever it suits him. Authority has been given to us to uphold God's Word, not to override it. Authority means that we have the full backing of all of heaven when we abide by the statutes given in Scripture but that we operate outside the bounds of that authority when we ignore God's Word or dismiss the witness of the Holy Spirit to our spirit.

God is the ultimate Authority and He has delegated the function of judging to Jesus who has in turn delegated the authority to His Word.[55] We have no right to unilaterally declare that the authority delegated to His church, His 'ekklesia', supersedes

His Word. In contemporary first century secular literature, 'ekklesia' referred to *a governmental assembly*. The church has the right, conferred by Jesus, to *bind* and *loose* in the manner of the judicial courts and legislative gatherings of His day. However, our right to *bind* and *loose* only applies to matters that are not already covered by His Word. Then we, as an 'ekklesia', get to decide together what is prohibited or what is permitted in particular circumstances. But nothing in those prohibitions or permissions should contradict either the Word or the Spirit that dwells within the Word—including the basic principles that reflect the unalterable character of God.

Now the circumstances surrounding the 'binding and loosing' protocol given by Jesus suggest that they are actually meant to be seen in contradistinction to the spellbinding of spirits. Jesus and His disciples were out in the wilderness at Caesarea Philippi, in front of the Gates of Hell at a shrine to the goat-god Pan. It was the Day of Atonement, the day on which a scapegoat was chosen by lot to be sent to the goat-demon Azazel out in the wilderness. The scapegoat carried the sin of the people back to the very demonic power to whom, by tradition, all sin is ascribed.

Jesus had gone out into the wilderness, to the temple complex of a goat-demon, thereby imaging Himself as the scapegoat. At the Gates of Hell, He says to Peter:

> *'I will give you the keys of the kingdom of heaven, and whatever you bind on earth shall be bound in heaven, and whatever you loose on earth shall be loosed in heaven.'*
>
> Matthew 16:19 ESV

Like so much else Jesus is involved with, these words resonate with the landscape and are, I suspect, meant to heal it. Overshadowing Caesarea Philippi was the snow-covered peak of Mount Hermon where Azazel and the Watcher angels had descended in the days before the Flood. There they had pronounced binding curses over one another to ensure none of them would renege on the plan to seek out beautiful human women as mates. The mountain itself was actually named for those binding curses. In addition, the Book of Enoch—an extra-biblical book that described the coming of the Watchers and that was immensely popular in first century Galilee—also related the binding of Azazel in an abyss in the wilderness. The Gates of Hell leading to an underground abyss would fit that description of an underground prison.

Binding curses were therefore part of that particular landscape. This is hardly surprising since sorcery—a combination of drugs and spellbinding—is Azazel's occult specialty. Jesus deliberately went into the very wilderness associated with the scapegoat, not to endorse the binding of spirits by words of power but to oppose it. In fact, He proclaimed a very different sort of binding: a *symphony*—the blended harmony that ideally comes from working together to establish a mutual agreement about church governance.[56]

Many people are reluctant to give up binding spirits for very pragmatic reasons: simply because it works. But who among its practitioners can guarantee that they've never crossed the line into the occult, given that the mode of operation today is so much closer to spellbinding than legislation? The fact that something works is no guarantee it's godly. Magic works. It works because it uses the creative power God instilled into words and the redemptive power He instilled into blood. But it uses them against Him and His purposes. Moreover, the devil is quite content to lose a minor skirmish and allow us to believe we have a technique that 'works' against him, so we become reliant on an unholy habit that will allow him to defeat us in the war. His strategies are diabolically cunning.

If you feel horrified reading this, good. You've understood how serious it is. If you've been practising binding and decide not to repent of it, but rather to continue, you need to be very sure that an exception has been made for you to exercise a practice that is nowhere sanctioned by the Word of God. And that exception cannot ever be decided by an individual.

The universe was made by the LOGOS, the Word of God, Jesus the poet and storyteller. It is both legal and lyrical in nature. It can be understood by means of science or through song—or preferably both. Logic fails at intervals in any investigation of creation because paradox is threaded through both the science and the song. It's comparatively easy to pursue the science but not so simple to follow the song. Yet one without the other leads away from the Singer.

Some people want the Word without the Spirit, and some people want the Spirit without the Word. Some people delight in steeping themselves in the well of the Word and some prefer to leave all that behind and ride the wind of the Spirit. A few want to drill deep into the etymology of particular Greek or Hebrew words, to unearth the most faithfully accurate meaning. But ultimately, for all that exactness, our understanding will be lopsided if we fail to consider that the divine Poet has shaped all words and that the resonances thrumming the air around the words are just as important as the meaning.

We need to get over our idolatry of scientific rationalism in the way we think and equally our idolatry of personal revelation. Both need to be held in tension. Because, paradoxically, our God is concerned on the one hand with meticulous precision in His Word and, on the other, with the evocation of tangential themes through subtle rhyme and playful puns.

I mention all this because I want to be clear about my non-standard approach to the understanding of Scripture: when I interpret words, I look at a combination of choices that involve some poetic nuances and a selection from a range of meanings. I'm aware some people are highly disturbed by this approach. One eminent scholar confessed to me that he detested it so passionately he had to look within himself to find the source of his loathing—and conceded that, while he agreed that God is an author and Jesus is a parable-maker and that Ephesians 2:10 says we are God's poetry, that wasn't how he was trained. He hated being drawn so far outside his comfort zone. None of his dictionaries of biblical words gave any consideration to head-rhyme or tail-rhyme, assonance, consonance, alliteration, allusion, puns or wordplay. How could he know the meaning of a word if a dictionary was just a starting point, not an endpoint? The answer to this, in my view, is obvious: follow the leading of the Holy Spirit.

With all this in mind, let's look at some Hebrew words to do with *binding* and *loosing—prohibiting and permitting—*and the spirits that are involved. The Hebrew for *bind* is 'asar' and for *loose* is 'sherah'. The additional senses of 'sherah' are *set free, sing,* and *remnant*; it is a very close assonance with *serve* and *minister* as well as *body armour* and *fortification.* And of course it rhymes with Asherah, one of the alternate names for the spirit of wasting. This tells us what Asherah's role was originally intended to be before she fell into corruption and, instead of assisting humanity as God intended, began to seek worship in her own right. Instead of binding us up, she was to help set us free, to enhance our singing, to support us in acts of service and ministering to God and others, to show us how to improve our fortifications and our armour.

Now *loosing* often brings a sense of *freedom*, precisely the heady feeling we experience when Python, the spirit of constriction, lifts the pressure. All too often at this point we relax our guard, thinking that the test and the attack is all over. Like Elijah after the climactic confrontation between Yahweh and the team of Baal-Hadad and Asherah, we allow victory to be wasted and swallowed up in defeat.

The Hebrew word 'rahab' comes from 'rachab', *broad of territory, roomy in every direction, made spacious, wide, spread out, proud.* The element, 'chab', within 'rachab' is related to 'chebel', *territory, cord, rope, band of companions.*

Now here's where we start getting poetic. The word 'chebel' is consonant with several words; but their relationship is actually deeper than simply the poetic. In *ancient* Hebrew, the spelling of 'chebel', *territory, cord, rope, band of companions* is identical with 'chabol' *pledge*, 'chobel', *sailor*, 'chibbel', *mast*, 'chabal', *hurt* or *injury*. These words are further related to 'chobelim', *union*, 'chebar', *company, association, spell* or *charm*, 'chabar', *unite, be joined, tie a magic knot* or *make a spell* or *charm*, 'chaber', *united, associate, companion*, 'chabar', *comrade*, and to 'Chebrown', Hebron, the name of a town of Judah meaning *association* or *league*.

There's a lot of positives and negatives in that line-up. And all of them should influence the way we understand the agenda behind the spirit of wasting, whether we call her Rachab or Asherah. Now a *band* and a *bind* are not in any way different—in fact, a *band* in English simply means *something that binds* or *is bound together*. The very fact we speak of a band of companions tells us that the group are tied together in the pursuit of a common purpose.

Ropes and *cords* bind things together, pledges bind people together, and hurt or injury inflicted by another person has binding power, if forgiveness is not brought to bear. *Sailors* of course use ropes—in fact, the ancient meaning of sailor was *rope-dancer*—and *masts* have ropes tied to them. It does seem odd, however, that the connotations of a ship's *mast* were more about what was tied onto it than as a wooden pole in its own right. But that might be explained by the fact a *mast* was one of the symbols of Asherah, the patron goddess of those rope-dancing sailors, and the deity who claimed the title 'She Who Walks On Water'. She was the ship that trod the waves and the protector of all those who sailed within her.

Several of the themes behind these words occur in the story of Rahab, the inn-keeper and prostitute of Jericho. The *pledge* of the two spies regarding her safety involves a scarlet *cord* or *rope* that she binds to her window as a sign of their agreement. The cord is described in Hebrew as a 'chebel'. However, that's not the only word used for it. It's also called 'tiqveh' which, besides signifying *cord*, can also mean *hope*. That one word with its built-in double meaning tells us it was a *rope of hope*.[57] In addition to 'tiqveh' and 'chebel', there's a third word used. This is 'chut', *line, thread* or *cord*. And to tie it all together—sorry, but that was an irresistible pun—is 'qashar', *binding, leaguing together, conspiring*. Perfect, not only because Rahab was indeed *conspiring* with the spies against the king of Jericho and the scarlet *cord* she *binds* to the window is the symbol for it, but because it reminds us of Asherah.

As the patron of sailors—not so much fishermen who kept close to shore, but rather those who voyaged across the high seas in trading ventures—Asherah is a sponsor of trading. The great sea port of Elath on the Gulf of Aqaba, an inlet of the Red Sea, where Solomon had a fleet of ships constructed is named after Asherah. The port is now called Eilat.

The name 'elath' derives from ''elat' and simply means *goddess* in the Canaanite language of Ugarit. In Hebrew 'elath' means *a grove of trees*. Asherah is linked to various kinds of trees: palm, oak, terebinth and tamarisk. Scripture mentions worship of 'the Asherah' and of Asherah poles. These may have been living trees that had carved figures in their bark or that had been trimmed to a particular shape. If they had been modified, they would have been considered both natural and 'made' or 'built'. It was forbidden to plant an Asherah tree next to an altar to Yahweh.[58]

In addition to *trees* as well as *masts* that doubled as Asherah poles, the iconography of Asherah also included deer, ibexes[59] and lions. She is called 'Mistress of Lions'—probably referring to her seventy sons, the so-called 'young lions'—and 'Mistress of Animals'[60] and also possibly 'Mistress of Fates'.[61]

I believe Asherah can be also identified as the spirit behind the woman mentioned in Revelation who is dressed in purple and scarlet and who sometimes sits on the seas and sometimes rides a hybrid leopard-bear-lion Beast. When the worship of Asherah was transferred to Babylon, she became Ashratum, 'Mistress of Voluptuousness and Joy.' She'd always been a fertility goddess but, in Babylon, she became associated with eroticism and luxury. The Book of Revelation describes the Whore of Babylon as opulently adorned, engaged in sexual immorality and thirsty for the blood of the saints.

> *One of the seven angels who had the seven bowls came and said to me, 'Come, I will show you the judgment of the great prostitute who is seated on many waters.'*
>
> Revelation 17:1 ESV

> *The angel said to me, 'The waters that you saw, where the prostitute is seated, are peoples and multitudes and nations and languages.'*
>
> Revelation 17:15 ESV

Just as the spirit of wasting calls up all the threshold guardians we've overcome individually to unite against us, so the Whore of Babylon will unite the kings of the earth[62] against the people of God. Now you may wonder how a goddess of fertility could be a spirit of wasting. Surely fertility is about abundance and fecundity—lush and rich fruitfulness. But consider for a moment: unless there's a shortage of these blessings, why would there be any need to worship the goddess? And if there's an issue more pressing than fertility, won't the people turn to a deity who claims to have the solution to that issue providing the right sacrifices are made? Asherah worship declined amongst the Canaanites when the Israelites arrived—the Canaanites turning instead to Asherah's daughter, the war-goddess Anat.

Waste and built-in obsolescence are integral to today's manufacturing sector. Where once appliances were robust and lasted four or five decades, now they are designed to fail after four or five years—preferably just after the warranty runs out. In the world of trade, people expect to pay more in times of shortage. Hence we see why Asherah can be both a spirit of wasting as well as fertility: in order to get people to agree to a sacrifice, there have to be shortages and waste to incentivise them to expend more of their strength and their resources in worship.

The Book of Revelation tells us that, eventually, the kings of the earth will turn on the Whore. They and the Beast who rose from the sea will hate her. The threshold guardians aren't natural allies. As fallen spirits they are not only innately enemies of God but of each other as well. They put aside their normal antagonism and combine forces against us when we prove to be a truly serious threat. And that only happens when we become committed to removing any obstacles in our lives between us and Jesus.

Once it becomes clear that we have unfettered access to the power of the atonement of Jesus, we raise our threat level to such a high degree that we have to be stopped. At any cost. Because we're starting to walk in our calling. That calling has a part specific to us as individuals and another part that is more general. One aspect of the general part is 'judging angels'[63] and, as these spirits know, we can have only one judgment in their case. A legal precedent is already set out for us in Psalm 82 so we know that mortality and death is the only sentence we can pronounce. This is why the threshold spirits are so desperate to stop us: they are immortal beings who do not want to taste mortality or death. This is also why, when we choose radical faithfulness to Jesus and keep pushing through covenant after covenant with Him, they seek external means to deny us access to the power of the atonement and thereby to waste all that we've achieved up to that point. It's about smashing our calling and stripping us of the inheritance we've been implementing and stealing back the mantle we've been given and allowing the assignment attached to the mantle to crumble into nothingness. If they can find a leader who has sufficient authority to speak into our lives and who is also willing to double bind us, then it's simply a matter of influencing that leader to put the death wrappings in place.

Double binding even happened to a leader as devoted to God as Joshua. If he had any misgivings about the orders he'd received from the Commander of the Army of the Lord for the taking of Jericho, they're not recorded. He obeyed anyway, despite their strangeness.

And because obedience was the condition for God's Terror, the Angel of War, to go before the Israelites and cause the hearts of the Canaanites to melt with dread so they'd be driven out, the battle of Jericho was a resounding victory. But then one of the Israelites disobeyed. Everything in Jericho was devoted to the Lord; there was a total ban on taking any spoils of war. But a man named Achan took a sumptuous robe from Babylon, along with a bar of gold and two hundred shekels of silver. In addition to this disobedience, there seems to have been a lack of diligence on Joshua's part. He took the word of the scouts sent to Ai that it was easy takings and apparently did not inquire of the Lord. The crack battalion sent against Ai was utterly routed and fled in panic.

The mop-up included identifying Achan as the one who'd violated the covenant, dealing with him and removing the defilement of the devoted things in the camp, then heading out to battle once more. It involved restoring covenant with God and bringing the people back into at_one_ment with Him. Once they had His covering back, they were again unstoppable.

You'd think after such a salutary lesson that Joshua would thereafter always inquire of the Lord. But he forgot. That isn't altogether surprising since the entire group of threshold spirits had obviously realised by this time that the Israelites were committed to obedience and a full frontal attack wasn't going to work. A workaround had to be found in order to double bind them and put obstacles in the way of their access to the atoning cover of God. Marshalling themselves, the threshold guardians found a group of local people willing to try to outwit Joshua and the Israelites by risking a deception. They were the Gibeonites. They arrived at the Israelite camp, displaying mouldy bread and worn-out sandals as evidence they came from a far country, and proposing a threshold covenant—that is, a covenant of defence—between themselves and the Israelites.

Now the Israelites had just reaffirmed covenant with God, so it was a psychologically opportune moment. Having just sworn oaths for one covenant, another might have seemed ideal. Maybe, in addition, there was some group mind control—a speciality of the spirit of abuse—going on.

Now God had told the Israelites not to make any treaties with the people of the land. A covenant of defence carries with it a mega-serious obligation to respond any time the covenant partner is in danger. It's such a major undertaking that Joshua and the elders really should have asked God before committing themselves. But they didn't. And the moment the covenant was ratified, they were in a double bind. They had two mutually opposing covenants—one with God and one with the Gibeonites. In a later age, David did the same—he had one covenant with Achish of the Philistines and contrary ones with Saul and Jonathan.

Joshua's covenant with the Gibeonites caused immediate difficulties for the Israelites and was still a source of trouble centuries later. On hearing that the Gibeonites had formed an alliance, a coalition of five neighbouring kings massed their armies and attacked them. The Gibeonites appealed for help to the Israelites and, fulfilling the covenantal promise of defence even though it was obtained through deception, Joshua and his army marched all night to surprise the attackers. The five kings fled and, conscious that he needed more time to finish the battle, Joshua famously called on the sun and the moon to stand still. The Gibeonites were saved and thereafter they became hewers of wood and drawers of water for the sacrifices in the Tabernacle. Nonetheless, the covenant between them and the people of Israel was a permanent fixture of society. It was now impossible for the Terror, the Angel of War, to fulfil his assignment and drive out all of the Canaanites. The covenant with the Gibeonites created a legal impediment to that mission.

Throughout the following centuries, the Gibeonites continued to show themselves masters of the technique of the double bind. David was caught in their manipulations. A long drought had occurred during David's reign and, desperate to end it, he inquired of the Lord regarding the cause. The answer came that it was because his predecessor Saul had massacred the Gibeonites and thereby violated the age-old covenant of defence. Now this event is never explicitly mentioned during the record of Saul's reign but, as I've indicated in *Dealing with Lilith*, I think the circumstances can be reconstructed. I believe the Gibeonites were accidental casualties in the battle between the Israelites and the Philistines that was started by Jonathan and his armour-bearer at Michmash Pass. That conflict eventually ranged over a huge swathe of territory as the Philistines fled along the road to the coast. In doing so, they passed Gibeon and would have been reinforced by their garrison there. Gibeon in the time of Saul was a cosmopolitan centre: the descendants of the Canaanites lived there, serving as labourers for the Tabernacle that was sited on a nearby hill; in addition, it was a Levitical city[54] and home to many priests who ministered in the Tabernacle; furthermore, the Philistines had a military outpost there. I think the most likely scenario is that the armies of Saul attacked the garrison at Gibeon, slaughtering anyone who was not clearly a Levite. As a consequence, many of the Gibeonites were killed, not deliberately or maliciously, but as 'collateral damage' in an active warzone.

Regardless of the reasons for the massacre, David was left with the spiritual aftermath. On discovering the cause, he went to the Gibeonites and asked them what they wanted to reverse the curse and bless the land. They wanted revenge on the House of Saul. This was the moment when they declared:

> *'It's not for us to execute anyone in Israel.'*
>
> 2 Samuel 21:4 ISV

They wanted David's permission for human sacrifice. And instead of inquiring of God whether breaking his own covenant with the House of Saul was an appropriate way to atone for a broken covenant by the House of Saul, David fell straight into the trap. The Gibeonites had no intention of blessing the land. They intended to extend the curse and to defile the Tabernacle in the process. By slaying Saul's sons and grandsons and leaving their bodies unburied, exposed on the Hill of the

Tabernacle, they added another double bind to the situation. God had commanded:

> *You must not leave the body hanging on the pole overnight. Be sure to bury it that same day, because anyone who is hung on a pole is under God's curse. You must not desecrate the land the Lord your God is giving you as an inheritance.*
>
> Deuteronomy 21:23 NIV

David couldn't punish the Gibeonites for their deception in activating a curse instead of a blessing without further covenant violation. Once again he did nothing when abuse became evident. Saul's concubine Rizpah was the only one who honoured the slain men—she protected their bodies from despoilation by birds of prey and wild animals. Everyone visiting the Tabernacle to pray about the drought would have seen her on the hillside as, for months, she conducted a harrowing, lonely vigil. But David wasn't amongst those supplicants. He'd become afraid.

> *The tabernacle of the Lord, which Moses made in the wilderness, and the altar of burnt offering were at that time in the high place at Gibeon. But David could not go before it to inquire of God, for he was terrified by the sword of the angel of the Lord.*
>
> 1 Chronicles 21:29–30 AMP

This is David, the man whose bold and fearless confidence in God had enabled him to single-handedly overcome a giant. The double bind made him petrified of approaching God in His Tabernacle. Remember there was no Temple at this point, so David was denying himself the comforts and benefits of the atonement. That's precisely what happens to us when others knot us into the death wrappings of double binds. We are denied access to the comforts and benefits of the atonement of Jesus.

Although Jesus is never recorded as binding a spirit, He speaks of binding the satan. He'd been accused by a group of Scribes of casting out demons by using diabolic power. Once again, we see some leaders trying to impose a double bind—not so much on Jesus Himself, as on the people. By declaring Jesus is in league with the enemy of all humanity and thus opposed to God, the Scribes ensured that ordinary people of faith would become reluctant to approach Him for healing. The deeper their devotion to God, the more confusion and hesitancy the leaders would have raised in their minds about Jesus. If the people—who are, of course, used to looking to the Scribes and Pharisees for spiritual guidance—decided the risk of disobedience to God is too great to go to Jesus, they were then denied the comforts and benefits of salvation—which includes healing. If they did go to

Jesus for healing, believing His power was a work of the devil, then they'd sinned for violating their conscience. It's the same-old-same-old strategy: put a double bind in place so that access to the full benefits of salvation are denied.

Jesus countered the claim of the Scribes with impeccable logic:

> *If a kingdom is divided against itself, that kingdom cannot stand. And if a house is divided against itself, that house will not be able to stand. And if Satan has risen up against himself and is divided, he cannot stand, but is coming to an end. But no one can enter a strong man's house and plunder his goods, unless he first binds the strong man.*
>
> Mark 3:24–27 ESV

Jesus wasn't declaring a binding over the satan at this point; He was saying that he is already bound. That's not a surprise because that's what happens as a natural part of the sowing-and-reaping cycle: if we bind others, we will suffer binding ourselves.

Jesus was warning the Scribes all through this encounter: you are declaring good to be evil, and evil to be good and thus binding up the people so they cannot lay hold of the goodness, love, mercy, grace, kindness and healing of God that has been stolen from them by the satan.

The labelling of good as evil and of Jesus as a satanic agent *so that others are deprived of salvation* is the sin against the Holy Spirit that will not be forgiven. We can be angry with God and think of Him as violent, judgmental and hate-filled and that can be forgiven. It's deliberately and knowingly stealing the blessings of salvation, including the calling of others, that won't be forgiven.

In a double bind, the effectiveness of the Fruit of the Spirit is minimised. LOVE cannot be actioned because there is simply no loving choice. Each is wrong. Whichever way we turn, Python has the situation sewn up. JOY is difficult to activate because we're trapped. PEACE is elusive, honour impossible. GOODNESS, KINDNESS and FAITHFULNESS are options no longer available to us. GENTLENESS simply doesn't come into the equation for either Jesus or, as we're about to see, for Phinehas either. PATIENCE will make no difference.

We can no longer rely on the Fruit of the Spirit as weapons—and there's a very good reason for our naked defencelessness in the face of the enemy. The Fruit matured in our lives as a result of passing various tests. In part, the Fruit are our own work of stewardship and obedience. But nothing of our own work is effectual against the enemy.

We have to rely solely on the atonement of Jesus—the very thing we are completely barred from accessing. But Jesus is not barred from it. He can open the way for us, using a whip if need be. But we have to choose Him, and we have to admit to Him that it's impossible for us to stop wanting to do something, anything, that will assist Him. The deep desire of our hearts is a perverted hope that we can somehow clean ourselves up, somehow remove all the legal rights of the enemy, somehow make God beholden to us through righteousness or obedience or tithing or good works.

In the dark recesses of our heart—the place that Jeremiah spoke of where the deceitfulness, wickedness and desperate corruption that is above all things is hidden[65]—we both hate God's grace and also feel entitled to it. We hate grace because we want to earn it. We want to earn the unearnable so that God is in our debt.

Only the atonement of Jesus can cure this incurable state of the heart.

Prayer

Loving Lord and heavenly Father,

I ask Your Holy Spirit to recall to my mind any times I have stepped outside the authority of Your Word and Your Will and instead chosen to exercise judgments and jurisdictions of my own devising that have not been delegated or assigned to me by You.

SELAH — PAUSE TO REFLECT.

I repent of those times, Lord. I repent of going outlaw. I repent of believing that I didn't need to know Your law because 'all authority' meant I didn't need to concern myself with such knowledge. I repent of ignoring the promptings of Your Holy Spirit who aided me even when I didn't have a clue about Your law and when everyone around me seemed to approve of something I felt deep conviction about participating in. I repent of honouring the leaders by my silence, and so dishonouring You.

SELAH — PAUSE TO REFLECT.

I ask Jesus to empower the words of repentance I've just spoken and, though His atonement, turn me around so that I uphold the authority of the Word of God. Keep me from dismissing the authority of Your Word and Your Spirit just because someone I respect is advocating a practice that goes against what is revealed in Scripture. Give me the boldness to ask what verses of Scripture they are basing their authority for that practice upon. Give me also the discernment to know whether their answer addresses the question I asked or was just designed to shut me up.

Remind me always to inquire of You, Lord. Don't let me forget until it's too late and I've unknowingly made an agreement with one of Your enemies. Prompt me at just the right moment with just the right question to ask. Forgive me for the times when Your Spirit did prompt me but I didn't ask. Help me navigate through the minefield that is in front of me, placed by Your adversaries and mine. Wake me up from my sleepy complicity with the evil one and show me Your plan for my redemption and for the salvation of my family—both my blood family and my family of faith. Show me how to partner with You, always keeping under Your authority, in working out that salvation in fear and trembling.

Kiss me with Your armour and help me stockpile Fruit against the attacks of the authorities and powers who oppose You.

I ask this is the name of Jesus of Nazareth.

Amen

6

Kinsman-redeemer

Whom God has mantled, no man can dismantle.

Facebook meme

IT'D BE WONDERFUL IF THAT social media meme were true. But I've seen too many thefts of divinely bestowed mantles to believe it. Perhaps *thefts* is not the right word. More like *shutdowns, deactivations, lockouts.* There's a serious attempt with a double bind to invalidate our calling and to cancel the assignment we were given when we were handed the mantle that is our faith inheritance.

Now when we see obvious attempts to double bind others, especially those who are our brothers and sisters in the faith, we are called to stand up for them. It's unfortunate that most people want to avoid confrontation and so go the Abraham-David route of doing nothing and therefore allowing wrong to escalate to intolerable levels. Through their complicity with the spirit of wasting, millennia of conflict ensued in Abraham's case, and civil war resulted in David's case.

The problem is that stepping in to defend another person caught in a double bind is almost always counterproductive and also results in complicity with the spirit of wasting. Before we look at how to avoid such an alliance, let's look at the spiritual dynamic involved in defending others in the family of faith.

When we step up and speak out for others, we are acting like a kinsman-redeemer from ancient times. A kinsman-redeemer was basically a family protector charged with the following duties:

(1) buying impoverished family members out of slavery or servitude.
(2) buying back any land that family members have been compelled to sell on a pro rata basis, bearing in mind the buyer would have had to relinquish the land in the year of Jubilee anyway.
(3) marrying the widow of a family member who'd died to give her security and to provide the deceased relative with an heir who would inherit any property in his name.[66] Both the marriage and the inheritance came together: a kinsman-redeemer could not claim the land holdings without marrying the widow.
(4) avenging the murder of a family member.

Normally the next-of-kin would have the role of the kinsman-redeemer. However it was possible to pass this duty on to another close relative who willing to take the duties on—as seen in the Book of Ruth. The responsibilities included preserving the dignity and welfare of the family, redemption of both land and people who are in trouble and bringing about atonement for a kin-slaying. In general terms, the kinsman-redeemer was a covenant defender.

The Hebrew word 'goel' means *kinsman-redeemer*. However, it also has another meaning: *defilement*. It may seem utterly strange that such a positive role can have such negative overtones. It's that last role—the avenger of blood—that gives us a sense of why these two seemingly disparate functions, *redeemer* and *defilement*, are associated with one another. Murder placed a curse on the land and the curse could only be lifted by the blood of the murderer.

> *Do not pollute the land where you are. Bloodshed pollutes the land, and atonement cannot be made for the land on which blood has been shed, except by the blood of the one who shed it. Do not defile the land where you live and where I dwell, for I, the Lord, dwell among the Israelites.*
>
> Numbers 35:33–34 NIV

The kinsman-redeemer in his role as the avenger of blood is directed to lift this curse on the land brought about by the murder of his relative. He must be willing to step into the curse and pursue the killer to avenge the blood on the land by the only available means: the blood of the murderer. Only the blood of one who shed blood can atone for the slaying and bring about peace with God.

Now, as far as I'm aware, there is only one example given in Scripture—apart from Jesus—of someone deliberately entering a curse. This specific case is described earlier in the Book of Numbers. It is such a significant passage that a close and careful look at what it says and doesn't say is necessary.

To set the scene: it's the fortieth year after the Israelites have left Egypt and they are once again on the threshold of the Promised Land. Decades previously, the report of ten spies had derailed the faith of the people and prevented entry into Canaan. The Israelites have been wandering in the wilderness ever since. Now, as they prepare to cross the Jordan, they have camped in the Valley of Acacias—the ancient site of Sodom and Gomorrah—and an even more serious issue threatens to derail their progress once more.

While in the Valley of Acacias, they encountered some Moabite and Midianite women who had been deliberately sent in by the king of Moab to seduce the Israelite men and invite them to ceremonies where they would worship Baal-Peor, *the lord of the opening*, and thus forsake their covenant with Yahweh. Now it's not as if the people don't know the punishment for such covenant violation is death. They do. There was a standard understanding across the ancient world, both inside Israel and out, both within nations and between nations, both for kings and commoners, both in the natural and in the supernatural. People knew that if you betrayed your covenant partner, you accepted the death sentence that was the consequence. That was what you'd agreed to when the covenant was cut in the first place. It was one of the curses that had been spoken over you and that you may even have spoken over yourself. Now obviously the men involved in this sacrilegious worship were banking on Baal-Peor being a mightier defender than Yahweh. Even though a plague—a sure sign that a covenant has been breached—broke out.

> *The Lord issued the following command to Moses: 'Seize all the ringleaders and execute them before the Lord in broad daylight, so His fierce anger will turn away from the people of Israel.'*
>
> *So Moses ordered Israel's judges, 'Each of you must put to death the men under your authority who have joined in worshipping Baal of Peor.'*
>
> *Just then one of the Israelite men brought a Midianite woman... right before the eyes of Moses and all the people, as everyone was weeping at the entrance of the Tabernacle. When Phinehas son of Eleazar and grandson*

*of Aaron the priest saw this, he jumped up and left the assembly. He took a spear and rushed after the man **into his tent**. Phinehas thrust the spear all the way through the man's body and into the woman's stomach. So the plague against the Israelites was stopped, but not before 24,000 people had died.*

Numbers 25:4–9 NLT

Now the English translations of the Hebrew in this passage are very curious. I have yet to find one that renders the emphasised words, *'into his tent',* adequately. The word for *tent* is extremely common in Scripture, occurring well over three hundred times. But in this instance, just this instance, only this once, a word that would normally be translated *curse* is used.

Phinehas obviously went into the tent but that's not what the Hebrew says. It says he went into the 'qubbah', *curse*, and then he put a spear through it. That's the meaning—because the word translated *stomach* is also derived from the same word for *curse*. In addition, while the Hebrew word 'naqab', related to 'qubbah', is not used in this section, it's implied. *To pierce* or *to curse* is the meaning of 'naqab'.

Now this reading entirely changes the way we see Phinehas' action. Superficially, when we read further into this passage, it's easy to get the impression that God rewarded a violent, vigilante action with amazing favour: an everlasting priesthood and a covenant of peace. But when we realise that Phinehas was willing to step into the curse, we see the foreshadowing of Jesus who took on the curse of sin for the entire world.

Phinehas was risking his life to stop the plague. Apparently he'd done a swift calculation that what it would take to atone for the covenant violation was three deaths. First, the execution of Zimri and Cozbi—the prince of the tribe of Simeon and the Midianite priestess—who'd just sauntered past the Tabernacle, flaunting their liaison and cocking a snook at God. They were openly treating the Lord with contempt and derision. The third death was his own for extra-judicial murder. He'd be breaking the law and could expect to be punished to its full extent. He has no right or authority to become judge, jury and executioner and do what he does. But God intervenes on his behalf.

Now, Phinehas is never described as a kinsman-redeemer but he certainly rises to assume the role of covenant defender. In doing so, he not only brings the plague to a halt and therefore saves the people but he also protects his great-uncle, Moses.

Take a close look at what God told Moses to do about the situation and what Moses relayed to the judges of the people. There's a significant difference. Moses actually changes God's instructions. It's not the only time that he passes on what God says through a filter of his own frustration and desire for control. Whereas God had directed Moses to execute the ringleaders,

Moses conveys this order to the judges as 'eliminate everyone involved.' This ruthless decree would have resulted in indiscriminate slaughter. Instead, the deaths of the two ultimate ringleaders who were removed by Phinehas was enough.

Herein we see God's justice and His mercy in balance. Covenant-breaking was the most serious of disruptions to relationship in the ancient world. Anyone who violated covenant could not be trusted. To not punish betrayal of covenant pledges was to invite complete social breakdown. It was to shred any prospect of justice, toss it aside and trample on the remains. However, to not see God's mercy in operation throughout this story is to miss the point. God's mercy extended to the people, to Moses and to Phinehas—each in different ways. God wanted those who had been the leaders in drawing others astray to be held responsible for the covenant violation and punished according to the known rules. He was not asking for everyone to be called to account, just those who'd led the rebellion.

When God ordered the execution of the ringleaders who led the people into betrayal of the covenant, it's not as if this was in any way cruel or unusual. It's actually merciful in making just the instigators of the covenant violation responsible and not everyone—which is what the people themselves would have expected as the punishment for treason.

Zimri, the prince of the tribe of Simeon, and the Midianite priestess Cozbi are provocative and brazen in their public stroll past the Tabernacle—they are not secretive about their liaison but openly bringing defilement into the camp. Their behaviour was inflammatory and dishonouring. They were flagrantly challenging God right outside His sanctuary. They were making the confrontation between Baal-Peor and Yahweh public; and their motive can only have been to prove that Baal-Peor's guard over them was so secure that Yahweh was impotent in the face of it. If they didn't believe they had Baal-Peor's protection and that it was greatly superior to that of the Lord God, they wouldn't have been so overtly defiant.

So Phinehas did not just stand up and save the people from the plague by his action, making atonement for the defilement brought in by covenant violation, he also stood up for God's honour.

God's balance of justice and mercy in this situation required the execution of just these two ringleaders who'd set themselves up as the champions of an idol and transformed a covenant breach into a contest between Baal-Peor's might and that of Yahweh.

Without Phinehas as covenant defender, the entry to the Promised Land may have been delayed again. He stepped into the curse and willingly put his life on the line. As a result God rewarded him with a covenant of peace and an everlasting priesthood for all his generations to come.

As we look at Phinehas' story today, we are apt to think that there's no need for a covenant defender, a kinsman-redeemer or an avenger of blood like him in our world. Society has changed. Civilisation has progressed. Any covenant violation by believers is taken care of by the atonement of Jesus.

True. Very true. However the principle of a family protector hasn't changed. While Jesus is our ultimate Covenant Defender, there are times when we need to be His spokesman and step up to the role of protector as well. Jesus is our Paraclete, as is the Holy Spirit—and 'paraclete' means more than comforter and advocate, consoler and intercessor. It has a legal sense of Defence Counsel and a military sense of Battle Companion. Both senses can be summed up as Covenant Defender.

God will sometimes call on us to image Jesus as covenant defenders and family protectors and guardians of our neighbours. (Remember the Good Samaritan?) Now our family today is not only one of blood but of faith as well. And while our church leaders and prophets would like to believe differently, they too can hear a message from God and transmit it, just as Moses did, with a great deal less accuracy than is desirable.

When that happens, God may ask us to intervene. He may call on us to stand up for fellow-believers who have been abused or betrayed and to defend them, taking on ourselves the role of a kinsman-redeemer. As a covenant defender, we are the voice of God and the voice of the voiceless.

It's interesting to note that, for some considerable time, the descendants of Phinehas were not beneficiaries of the everlasting priesthood that accompanied his covenant of peace. In the period that extended from before the birth of Samuel through to the end of the reign of David, the descendants of Ithamar, the uncle of Phinehas, came to be the high priests of all Israel. Eli, the high priest who confronted Hannah in Shiloh, was a descendant of Ithamar.[67] The last high priest from the House of Eli was Abiathar who was attached to David's court even before he was king. Abiathar was removed by Solomon from his office and exiled for supporting Adonijah, Solomon's elder half-brother, in his bid for the throne. Zadok, the priest who replaced Abiathar and anointed Solomon king, was descended from both Phinehas and Ithamar.

This is an overall curious development in the story of Phinehas, given the unconditional promise of God. The reasons for it happening are completely unknown, however rabbinical tradition offers some intriguing possibilities regarding the temporary displacement of his sons and grandsons as high priests:

- Phinehas did not provide Torah instruction to the armies of Israel prior to the battle at Gibeah.
- Phinehas did not nullify the vow made by Jephthah and thereby save Jephthah's daughter.
- Phinehas did not prevent the war between Jephthah and the men of Ephraim.

The last two seem to be a very long stretch since Phinehas would have had to have lived to over three hundred years of age to have still been alive during the era when Jephthah was a judge in Israel. However, the first is a possibility, since it is within the lifetime of Phinehas. Moses had instructed the people that the priest 'anointed for war'[68] was to encourage the people that God was with them:

> *When you are about to go into battle, the priest shall come forward and address the army. He shall say: 'Hear, Israel: Today you are going into battle against your enemies. Do not be fainthearted or afraid; do not panic or be terrified by them. For the Lord your God is the one who goes with you to fight for you against your enemies to give you victory.'*
>
> Deuteronomy 20:2–4 NIV

The priest anointed for war was the one who led out the armies, blowing a silver trumpet and holding holy articles. Phinehas is described as carrying this out during the war against Midian that immediately follows God's gift of a covenant of peace to him.[69]

Now, regardless of whether they are right or wrong, the Hebrew sages obviously followed a singular line of thought in coming up with these three possibilities. The rationale behind their understanding is extremely interesting—in their view, Phinehas, the covenant defender of the people, failed to continue in his mission of covenant defence. He was at some point derelict in duty. Therefore, his descendants were unable to follow him into the high priesthood for several centuries.

It follows that, in rabbinical understanding, we simply can't decide to take the role of covenant defender one day and then drop it the next. That's a complete compromise of the integrity that is built into the covenant of peace. In taking on any assignment involving covenant defence, we need to be aware that we will often be in the position of safe-guarding the abuser as well. By pointing out that their actions do not align with the will of God, we are trying to get them to understand the need to come back under the shelter of God's protective covering.

Importantly, to be able to take on this defender role, we need to be willing to step into a curse. And that curse may be heading our way from several directions: from the abuser, from church leaders with more sympathy for the abuser than the victim, from the violence that permeates the home or the sanctuary, from the defilement on the land crying out for healing.

Anyone called to the role of covenant defender, and who is willing to take it on, needs to ask God for a covenant of peace.

Otherwise, our defence may become vengeful in nature and closer in spirit to toxic enabling than to bringing the atonement of Jesus into the situation so reconciliation can occur and truth, mercy, justice and peace—the four elements of the kiss of heaven and earth[70]—all blend in perfect balance.

Several times in my life I've confronted a Christian leader who was trying to discard a team member from a particular voluntary position. It was not that any of these team members had done anything wrong to deserve expulsion, the leader just wanted them gone, despite their experience and expertise. One leader had found someone who, in his view, had a 'better look' to fill the role. He was simply going to replace the woman who'd given several years of her life in service to his team. He couldn't understand why I objected to his plan or why I told him rewarding faithfulness with rejection and valuing glamour more than reliability was inappropriate for a Christian leader.

In my naïvety, I thought he'd be grateful when I came up with an idea to save the woman from rejection and him from enacting a cruel and heartless decision. There would be no need to demote her or push her out because I'd invite her to help me pioneer a special project. The woman was, of course, thrilled for her talents to be recognised and, once reassured that accepting my offer wouldn't create a hole regarding the work she was already doing, immediately came on board with the project.

Like I said, I was naïve. And not just once either. Every single time. I could put my gullibility down to the mind control operating in these types of situations, but that doesn't entirely explain my repeated lack of wisdom. Whenever a similar situation happened and I prayed about the matter and thought up what I considered was an ideal solution to someone's insensitive expulsion by a leader, I foolishly believed the leader would be grateful for a way out. In retrospect, I'm astonished at my own credulity. Eventually I realised something was really wrong. Really, *really* wrong. In every single instance where I'd tried to defend someone, any relationship I'd had with the leader crumbled irretrievably shortly afterwards. Moreover, the person I'd tried to help had lost their faith at the same time. I'd thought I'd facilitated a side-stepping of the rejection, the dishonour, the prejudice, the humiliation and the injustice that the leader proposed to mete out. Instead all I did was delay the avalanche. The fruit that had developed out of my attempts at defence was so bad, it could only be classified as evil.

Now if I'd known that covenant defenders are stepping into curses, I might have known how to pray about all these very different situations. I might have asked for a covenant of peace. But, in fact, I'd taken one look at the story of Phinehas receiving the covenant of peace and I'd said to God, 'No, thank You. I'd really prefer not to enter into a curse. I'd be more than happy if four covenants came my way. I don't need any more than blood, name, threshold and salt.' That was my attitude every time I thought about the covenant of peace—not for me. Definitely out of my league. I'm not cut out to be like Phinehas, I'd tell Him. I don't have that kind of courage and I certainly don't need any more curses than I've already got.

Still, having catalogued the fruit of particular situations under the label of *evil*, I set out to research what that classification actually meant. It's one thing to have a subjective opinion that certain circumstances display the characteristics of evil, but it's another to have an objective tickbox-list to use as a guide. I set out to find that tickbox-list. The best that I've come across is in Ted Peters' book, *Sin: Radical Evil in Soul and Society*.

He outlines the process of descent into evil in seven steps:

(1) ANXIETY
(2) UNFAITH
(3) PRIDE
(4) CONCUPISCENCE
(5) SELF-JUSTIFICATION
(6) CRUELTY
(7) BLASPHEMY

Some of these steps need explanation and they don't necessarily follow each other in the exact order given. This is just the usual way that people choose to progress through the seven levels, but it can be different for some individuals.

Briefly, ANXIETY is, according to Peters, not sinful in itself but it readies us for a decision to choose evil rather than good. He uses the unusual term, UNFAITH, to express a condition much deeper than doubt and to carefully differentiate it from doubt. UNFAITH refers to a catastrophic loss of faith.

CONCUPISCENCE is lust for power. It refers to the desire to dominate others—sexually, socially, spiritually, psychologically, physically, emotionally, financially—in any way coercive control can be exercised. BLASPHEMY, although technically the right word, is probably better categorised as the transposition of good and evil (yes, that sin against the Holy Spirit Jesus referred to) and involves the inversion of spiritual symbols. That is, a symbol with a good meaning is invested with a poisonously bad meaning. Consequently, the spiritual comfort that should be available to people becomes so tainted, it is a source of trauma rather than blessing.

Thus I'd reword Peters' list to be a little clearer:

(1) ANXIETY
(2) CATASTROPHIC LOSS OF FAITH
(3) PRIDE
(4) DESIRE FOR DOMINATION
(5) SELF-JUSTIFICATION
(6) CRUELTY
(7) SYMBOL INVERSION

By the time any leader has got down to self-justifying cruelty, matters are at an incredibly serious stage. Such a leader stands on the very cusp of the last step into evil—BLASPHEMY: calling evil 'good' and good 'evil'. Leaders may be able to hide their anxiety as well as their loss of faith and desire for domination behind a hypocritical façade. However, once they begin to excuse their deliberate wounding of others, then it's obvious that pride and lust for power is lurking behind the scenes regardless of any charming front they present to the world.

It may not be possible for a covenant defender to hold back the evil pounding at the gates like a battering ram. Too many leaders have surrounded themselves with people who will agree with their plans for harming others. The supporters buy into the excuses and, rather than join the defence force, they open the gates so that the battering ram doesn't smash the barrier and wreck it. It's simply treason against God from within the church.

The leader who is perpetrating evil sees anyone who protests the mistreatment of the victim as an enemy. So do the leader's supporters. Abuse now spreads from the victim to the covenant defender and then further to the associates of the covenant defender. Neither the leader nor his supporters are able to recognise the neutrality of the covenant defender's position. Anyone who is not for them in terms of total submission and unquestioning loyalty is an adversary. In fact, the covenant defender became an adversary at the moment they refused to be dominated.

The covenant defender is effectively a paraclete, a mediator, a kinsman-redeemer, an armour-bearer, a battle companion, who hopes to bring about a reconciled relationship between the leader and the victim. Now that I've been through several situations like this, I can see the pattern and draw up the parallels between them and understand why the role of covenant defender is difficult to the point of impossible.

The leader treats the covenant defender as an opponent, rather than a helper, and so will not communicate in a timely way, dribbling relevant information even when asked for all pertinent material. Just before an advertised event, the leader will announce that plans have been altered and it will become clear the changes were contemplated even before the approved advertising went out. The key changes will only affect the victim, the covenant defender and their associates. The timing will be too late for advertisements to be amended. There will no apology for dishonouring the group affected, for the sudden changes, for the lateness of the disclosure to them or for keeping them out of the communication loop.

As those affected scramble to enact the changes and reel from each disclosure as it's trickled out bit by bit, destruction of trust ensues. The victim might not have had a high view of the leader but, generally speaking, the covenant defender and associates had been extending the benefit of the doubt to the leader and hoping it was all a misunderstanding. That's now gone and the erosion of trust is exacerbated by the leader separating himself or herself from anyone other than his supporters for meal times, prayer times, Bible studies and even worship. Lies about finances are exposed.

Lastly and most significantly of all, there will be an inversion of a symbol associated with covenant. A defilement of covenant will occur.

- It could be about a covenant meal, allegedly open to all, but publicised to just a few.
- It could be about covenant rest—a refusal by a leader to schedule time off for his team, even a Sabbath, while he takes what he wants at his convenience.
- It could be about covenant prayer—setting a time with a church member to pray with them for deliverance and then forgetting the appointment, not just once but several times over a period of more than a year, while never apologising for not

keeping the commitment.

- It could be about covenant freedom—the leader sets a person free by publicly refusing her the freedom to associate with those he disapproves of, and also banning her from blowing a shofar with its sound of freedom.
- It could be about covenant holiness—the leader is able to speak and behave profanely in a worship service but any question as to whether his actions are appropriate is immediately shut down. The leader is not, in his view, dishonouring God; but it is dishonour of him to suggest he was.
- It could be about covenant hospitality—the leader sends out invitations to a gala for the laying of the cornerstone for a new project, but the major donors are not included.
- It could be about covenant protection—the leader, on being informed of abuse, makes the informant the problem to be removed, not the abuser.
- It could be about covenant friendship—instead of keeping confidence, as friends do and as privacy laws require, the leader routinely betrays privileged secrets disclosed during counselling and also identifies the person who shared the secrets.
- It could be about covenant inheritance—the leader shuts down any opportunity for others to exercise their calling and tries to strip them of their mantle. In extreme cases, a board may decide to discipline a ministry's designated

heir-apparent for being too pastoral and not sufficiently CEO-like, forcing them out of the very ministry they've been appointed to lead on the death of the founder.

Now I've described each of these as *covenantal* in nature, and that's what they are. There's more to them than just simply a meal or a prayer or a gossip session or a power grab. There's a deep spiritual component to every one of these situations involving a perversion of God's intention for covenantal oneness.

Now, although I've mentioned a theft of covenantal inheritance last in the list above, each of the violations I've mentioned was in fact a precursor to the seizure of the fullness of the covenantal inheritance God wanted for each person. Their calling was snatched away by trauma and breach of trust. Eventually the moment comes when both the covenant defender and the one being defended recognise betrayal. The reaction is often visceral—a feeling of disbelief, of being stunned, nauseated, heartsick, grief-stricken, shattered. It often takes years to recover.

Covenant is about oneness. God means for us to be one Body under one Head, so these attacks on covenant are attacks on oneness. Excluding a member of the Body is like amputating a hand. But that's alright for most leaders—barring, of course, the one focussed on the covenant freedom who makes us free by refusing us permission to leave his church so that we don't get enslaved by the ideologies of others.

Because it is an attack on covenant, and therefore on oneness, by a leader to whom loyalty and trust has been given and who carries in their position an image of God as a king, the victim is in danger of losing their faith. The covenant defender, first and foremost, needs to pray for them, so this doesn't happen.

It's vital to remember every single attack that is orchestrated by the spirit of wasting in concert with all the other threshold spirits has a single purpose. Each and every double bind is there to deny us access to the atonement, shatter our faith and tie us up in death wrappings that will prevent us from obtaining the full benefits of salvation—peace, health, wholeness, integrity, completeness, soundness, welfare—the *shalom* of God.

The ultimate goal of the spirit of wasting is that we lose our faith. That will not only undo all the good that we've done but it will ensure we've turned away from our calling and are no longer the slightest threat to the powers of darkness.

When we think of all the people who have been wounded by church leaders, and have then left to practise a private faith, assuming they have any left at all, we can see how remarkably successful the double bind strategy is. Decades later, the victims are still trapped by the death wrappings and have long since ceased to struggle against them.

All too often, the final breach with the leader comes when they say, 'If you disobey me, you disobey God.'

This is an expression of *Covering Theology*.[71]

So why do leaders not mature in the Fruit of the Spirit as time goes on? Why do they not draw closer to God but further away? There are many reasons and, of course, these are not confined to leaders. There's a refusal to acknowledge, confess and repent of any of the following:

- the passivity of Abraham when it comes to abuse
- the communication spin of Moses when it comes to hearing from God
- the apostasy of Solomon when it comes to worship
- the defiance of Elijah when it comes to completing a divine assignment
- the self-justification of David when it comes to interpreting the Lord's favour
- the memorial-building of Saul when it comes to a name
- the opportunistic cruelty of Joseph when it comes to stewarding the inheritance of others
- the deceit of Jacob when it comes to wealth and assets
- the irresponsibility of Jonah when it comes to discipling others who've repented

- the negligence and elitism of Elisha when it comes to preaching the gospel to outsiders

Any one of these has the potential to bring about the fall of a leader. Yet instead of getting help for a weakness, the leader excuses it 'because we're all sinners.'

Unfortunately, 'But we're all sinners' can become the rationalisation for rebellion, lack of repentance and a mantra for the covering of shame. Jesus is meant to be our covering, not a cliché.

'But we're all sinners' can be the expression of a self-imposed double bind—an interior one rather than an externally imposed one. If that's the case, it's a spit in the face of Jesus as it ignores 'saved by grace' and what such salvation really means. Instead of appropriating the means God has offered us to draw nearer to Him, it says, 'I'm quite comfortable where I am. I desire no further access to the atonement of Jesus. I'm covered just enough and I have pretty much what I want.'

This is not conscious, of course, but it's one of the major ways leaders can close down their own access to the atonement—all the while claiming to be, either by word or action, the covering for those they should be shepherding and guiding to safe pastures. Make no mistake about it: 'covering'—whether it is implicit in a hierarchical structure or explicit in a claim that we need to be unconditionally obedient to a leader in order to receive blessings and avoid curses—is an assertion that the atonement of Jesus is not all-sufficient and that there needs to be another intermediary to help Him out.

Let's be very clear: we do not atone. Jesus has done that. If we're called to the role of a covenant defender, we facilitate an introduction to the atonement. That's the limit of what we can do and to try to take on any more is to usurp the role of Jesus. We might act *like* a kinsman-redeemer but it is beyond us to offer true salvation. We can only point to its source in Jesus. To try to take on the sin, the reaping, the disease, the punishment or the grief of others is effectively to tell Jesus His atonement is not enough and we're here to help Him out.[72] Fleshly pity, ungodly empathy and unholy compassion for the pain and suffering of others can tempt many of us to get in the way of Jesus so that we are the saviour, not Him. Yes, we might be called to mediate but only in as far as we can direct others to the Wonderful Mediator—Jesus Himself—the only One who can bridge the gulf between heaven and earth. When we encourage others to choose a false refuge or a coping mechanism ahead of, or instead of, Jesus our priestly mediator, we are declaring our own lack of belief in the atonement. While it's actually our faith that is deficient, we've turned it around in our thoughts so we secretly believe the work of Jesus on the Cross is deficient.

Now once leaders have shut down their own access to the atonement through some excuse for lack of repentance, they will ultimately lose both spiritual power and authority. For a time, it may actually seem as if their power increases, while God tries to draw them back—but that will eventually pass. They'll soon notice they've dropped their mantle. That's when they start to look around to see if they can pick up someone else's mantle to make up for the loss. Instead, they should be humbly asking Jesus to retrieve the inheritance they've lost, mislaid or forfeited, inquiring of Him how it was they drifted so far from Him and how it came about that they made no effort to seek rescue. And then, request that He, through the atoning power of His blood, rights their course.

'We're all sinners' should be a rallying cry to return to Jesus and allow Him to defeat sin in us through the power of His atonement. It should not be a pretext for denying the transformational power of the atonement in our lives but it should be an invigorating challenge to lay hold of the atonement and all that has been won for us at the Cross.

Immediately after Phinehas is granted a covenant of peace and the plague has stopped, God gives this direction to Moses:

> *Attack the Midianites and execute them, because they've acted deceitfully, bringing trouble to you in this incident at Peor with*

> *Cozbi, daughter of a prince from Midian, who was killed during the plague that came about because of the incident at Peor.*
>
> Numbers 25:17–18 ISV

In contrast to the mercy just shown to both Phinehas and the Israelites, this extreme judgment on the Midianites seems unbearably harsh. But given the status and importance of covenant in the ancient world, what the Midianites did was much more reprehensible than what the Israelites did. The Midianites purposefully set out to destroy the intimacy of the marriage relationship between Yahweh and the Israelites.[73] They schemed to get the Israelites to betray their marriage vows, to break covenant and call down curses upon themselves.

This is a declaration of war on a far higher level than normal. It's an attack on God by luring His Beloved into being unfaithful to Him. Now the relationship between Yahweh and the Israelites had had its fair share of rocky moments in the previous forty years. However, this is a whole different ballgame. But it's not a new ballgame—after all, a conspiracy against the covenantal relationship between God and His people should call to mind the machinations of the serpent in Eden.

And as we think of the story of Adam and Eve, we once again see a stark contrast in God's reactions. There's a promise of redemption and deliverance for humanity, but not for the fallen angels. Now, in my view, the reason for this difference is simple: Adam and Eve did not set out to betray God. It happened and it was a deliberate choice but their disloyalty wasn't intentionally planned, pre-meditated or calculated. They fell into a trap.

Similarly, the Midianites set out and baited a snare, colluding with Balaam—who was killed in the ensuing war[74]—to bring about the downfall of the Israelites by enticing them to destroy their covenant with God. Covenant violation is vile enough. But to devise a deliberate temptation to induce another person to violate covenant is so serious God will not countenance it continuing on further. Nor will He countenance it being repeated.

The parable of Jesus directed at Caiaphas, the rich man dressed in purple who had five brothers, is basically a warning about a similar matter: 'You're going to hell, Caiaphas.' Caiaphas didn't just tempt people to violate covenant with God as the Midianites did, he compelled it. He refused to release the Jews of the first century from the double bind he and his collaborators had contrived. All that was necessary to facilitate an unbinding was a choice of a half-shekel coin from a different mint.

From these three stories—the fallen angels, the Midianites and Caiaphas—we see that God doesn't tolerate double binds and deal gently with the offenders who set them up. Leaders who do so have declared war on God and on God's people. And if it's war they want, it's war they get. The violence of the outcome reflects the violence done in disrupting the intimacy of God with His Bride through denying access to the atonement.

God's righteous anger is implacably directed towards those whose desire for control is so great they conspire to cause others to sin. He withdraws His mercy from those schemers who plot to compel others to engage in dishonour, or open themselves to demonic powers or violate their own conscience, and thus be deprived of the benefits and blessings of salvation as well as any ability to exercise their calling.

Prayer

Loving Father,

I forgive those who were in authority over me or to whom I gave power who have robbed me of dignity and humiliated me by putting me in a double bind.

I forgive those leaders who have dishonoured me and manipulated me by putting me in a double bind.

I forgive those leaders who have used my talents to serve their agenda instead of God's purposes by putting me in a double bind.

I forgive those leaders who have stolen my agency, making me responsible for my actions while depriving me of choice through a double bind.

I forgive those leaders who have denied me freewill and the sanctity of my own conscience through a double bind.

I forgive those leaders who muzzled my voice and asked for my silence, and tried to use my mantle to replace theirs through a double bind.

I forgive those leaders who demanded submission without mutuality and who acted like tyrants, not servant-kings, through putting in place a double bind.

I forgive those leaders who took away my ability to bless and to be a blessing through a double bind.

I forgive those leaders who divested me of the ability to be blessed by God, by denying me access to the atonement through a double bind.

I forgive those leaders who sacrificed me because they did not believe in the atonement and so enacted a double bind.

I forgive myself for believing that any authority had the right to act so abusively simply because they were an authority.

In choosing to speak these words of forgiveness, Father, I ask that Jesus—through His atonement—empower them to truly achieve the release and pardon I have declared. I ask His blood to speak to my heart and cause true forgiveness to bloom there, just as I have spoken.

Father, I repent of the times I simply accepted the double bind and the violation of conscience that came with it.

I repent of the times I chose to keep quiet in order to keep my favoured position or to avoid the retaliation I saw others experience.

I repent of my false loyalty in granting to leaders an allegiance that should only be given to You.

I repent of not stepping up and speaking out in covenant defence of others who I knew were innocent of the accusations against them.

I repent of being complicit with the threshold spirits influencing the leaders and of not attempting to protect them from themselves.

I repent of not believing the atonement of Jesus is all-sufficient for the situations I've faced.

I repent of granting wasting access to my life and to my family.

In choosing to speak these words of repentance, Father, I ask that Jesus—through His atonement—empower them to truly achieve the change and return to You that I have declared. I ask His blood to speak to my heart and mind and cause true repentance to grow strong there, just as I have spoken.

Father, I renounce any invitation I or my ancestors have given to the spirit of wasting and all her allies, under whatever names they've assumed, to be part of my life and that of my family. I ask that Jesus be my Covenant Defender and forbid any retaliation by these spirits. Father, I ask that You rebuke them. I ask that Jesus of Nazareth revoke any covenant I have with any of these spirits and that these covenants and all the curses and clauses associated with them be cancelled at the Cross of Jesus. I ask that all copies of these covenants be retrieved by Your recording angels and destroyed completely at Your direction. Guard my heart from the spirit of wasting from now on.

I ask for forgiveness from You, Lord, for saying *no* to any covenants that You offered to me in the past where I misunderstood the love, grace and purpose of Your gift. Ask me again, please. Grant to me at Your appointed time the entire fullness of all the covenantal onenesses with You, with Jesus, Your Son, and with the Holy Spirit.

In the name of Jesus of Nazareth, my Covenant Defender and Kinsman-Redeemer.

Amen

7

Against the Cabal

The highest fortress hides
the deepest hurt,
the strongest tower defends
the darkest pain.
Thick walls, long-built, protect
the lonely heart
far out upon this scarred and barren plain.

Invincible these gates
to guile or stealth,
these stony parapets
are stormed in vain.
Hope's locked within, quite safe
from any lure.
Is there no chance we can build trust again?

If ——
with seven-fold love,
I come patiently round—
and round, and round,
and patiently round—
and round, and round,
and patiently round—
will your walls,
My child,
come tumbling down?

Anne Hamilton
The Walls of Jericho

CS Lewis, writing in his early poetry under the pseudonym Clive Hamilton, describes a dark mother, the watcher in every door. Ephesian Artemis is the description he gives her, though she has as many names as there are nations who follow after her.

She is the one who sits enthroned on the waters, who rides a beast with seven heads. The waters are, as we've previously seen, peoples, multitudes, nations and languages. The seven heads are seven hills and the woman is a great city that rules over and commands the allegiance of the great leaders of the earth.

In *Dealing with Lilith*, the correspondence of people and places is discussed at length. We are persons and places. We are the New Jerusalem and the Temple of the Holy Spirit. Likewise, throughout the Scriptures, spirits are both beings and places.

The dark mother is a harlot, a trader in covenants, the spirit of wishing who tempts us to wish instead of pray, to trade with Sheol or bargain with the threshold guardians or even try to transact with God instead of hope in Him and rely on the grace that overflows the atonement of Jesus.

She is Asherah, the mother of seventy young lions who are the spirit-princes of the nations. She is the one who allegedly treads the sea, walks on water, rides the waves and drives the dragon of the deeps.[75] One interpretation of her name is *tread*, thus she will try to lay hold of God's promise to us that wherever the sole of our foot treads is our inheritance. She's therefore in league with her daughter Anat, the spirit of dispossession, as they attempt to seize our inheritance in Christ, and lay waste to what He has given us to possess as His stewards. It is up to us to cooperate with the Terror, God's angel called War, to drive her out.

Asherah is also perhaps 'Lady Day', *goddess of the day*, and her pride of young lions is a company of light. She is called 'Holy One'. Her name sounds like 'ashira', *I will sing*.

In Iranian stories, Asherah walks on water, gives birth to seventy deities, and also teaches carpentry and brick-laying. Her symbols are lions, lilies, a tree, a cross, lions and ibexes or a triangle on a pole. Another of her symbols is a mast or upright pole, allegedly because her name means *straight*—in addition to *tread*.

In the Baal Cycle of Ugarit, the gods usually turn their faces to wherever they want to go and simply arrive. However Asherah is mounted on a donkey, led by a servant and followed by a troupe of minor deities. This may be an indicator of her status and rank within the Canaanite pantheon—it is thought perhaps it is not fitting for her to arrive without a processional.

The middle element of her name is 'shor', the *umbilical cord* which is regarded as a centre of strength. This is of course related to the navel. On gold amulets from Ugarit featuring Asherah, she is depicted with a pronounced navel with a tree etched on it. The Hebrew word 'shor' is, very strangely, derived from *enemy* or *treacherous watcher*. In the story of Rahab, the inn-keeper of Jericho, the word used for *binding the scarlet cord to the window* has the sense of *treacherous watcher*.

When we compare Asherah to Rahab, we see several parallels. Asherah is called *great*, 'rab', one of the more subtle nuances of 'rahab'. Both are harlots, both are traders, both are willing to bargain for covenants. As Asherah, the goddess most revered by the Canaanites at the time, was being evicted by the Terror, so Rahab reports that the hearts of the people of Jericho have melted in dread of the Israelites. God's hornet has indeed gone before them to drive out their enemies. And though the Israelites don't tread on water as Asherah claims to do, they 'pass over' the Jordan when the waters roll back and heap upstream near a town called Adam.

After two defeats—Jericho and Ai—the spirits who have been dwelling in the land God has reserved for Himself rouse themselves in an alliance against the incomers. God had chosen the family of Abraham as it descended through the sons of Jacob as His own special people and He had also chosen the land of Israel as their inheritance. These He had kept for Himself after the rebellion at Babel, while handing over the governorship of the nations to seventy principalities, the angel-shepherds who were appointed as rulers of the world beyond that tiny preserve where God had chosen to put His name.[76] Asherah and her young lions were unhappy at the prospect of complete expulsion. So they had to find a way to ensure it could never ever happen. A double bind involving an everlasting covenant was the perfect solution. And so they sent in the Gibeonites.

Throughout the ages, the double bind has been the weapon of the cabal. It's designed to bring down and lay waste to all we've achieved in getting over the threshold and into our calling. Notice how it's only when Joshua and the Israelites are actually in the Promised Land that this strategy is deployed.

Every externally imposed double bind is designed to deny us access to the atonement of Jesus and to the blessings of our covenant with Him. Once we're trapped by it, whatever we do is wrong. We cannot avoid dishonouring God. Once the Israelites had agreed to the covenant with the Gibeonites, they were in strife.[77] It didn't matter whether they kept the agreement or not—violating a covenant was abhorrent to God, but keeping it was just as abhorrent because He'd told them not to make any treaties with the people of the land. Similarly in the time of Jesus, the Temple tax was a double bind: if the men didn't pay the atonement tax, they disobeyed a command of God, but if they did pay the tax with a blasphemous graven image on a coin, then they were mocking God.

Apart from the double binds those who have power over us put in place, there are other bindings we need to deal with.

- Trauma bonds between ourselves and the perpetrator need to be severed in prayer, in much the same way as soul ties need to be cut. If a leadership *group* is involved, not just a *single* leader, it is appropriate to cut spiritual ties with different pairings and sets of individuals as well as the leader.
- Unforgiveness also forms a bond that can only be released through forgiveness.
- The bonds of false loyalty also need to be renounced.

Now the nature of double binds is such that, if a leader is unwilling to release us and, if resigning so that they now longer have power over us to enforce the double binds is not an option, then we have three alternatives. There may be more, but these are the ones I've discerned at the time of writing:

- We can invite Jesus to plait a whip and come into the situation to overturn the trading that the leaders have engaged in with respect to our lives, callings and destinies. They have substituted trading for covenant, blocked our access to the atonement, tried to use our loyalty against us and sought to gain our mantles to replace the power they have lost. If we choose this option, chaos and disruption will ensue and it's wise to ask Jesus for protection against the death threats that will come against our names, reputations, job and position—as well as those of our friends and family.

- Alternatively, we may sense that our situation is more like that of Lazarus: encased in death wrappings and hidden away in a cave-tomb behind a huge immovable stone that is beyond our strength to shift. So, in this instance, we ask Jesus to command His angels to move the stone aside and to then direct, 'Unbind him and let him go.' Ask Him also that the bindings are burnt away so that they cannot be used again against anyone else and so that any defilement of decay clinging to them is destroyed. Once again, it's wise to ask Jesus for protection against the death threats that will come against our names, reputations, job and position—as well as those of our friends and family.

- Thirdly, we can choose to ask for a covenant of peace to protect us as we go in to bat for another person and defend them against a superior. This is not support in a general sense; it's specifically protection against abuse. Bear in mind that, despite the term 'covenant of peace', we are stepping into a curse so there is the potential for violence. Yet again, it's extremely wise to ask Jesus for protection against the death threats that will come against our names, reputations, job and position—as well as those of our friends and family.

There are two gifts we need from the Lord in all this: vigilance and rest. They may seem at odds, they may seem too paradoxical to be practical. Yet an attitude of alertness, wakefulness and clarity of mind combined with an outlook of stillness, quiet waiting and gentle repose is just what we need. Only Jesus can give us such transcendent calmness combined with careful watchfulness. Because, the entry into His rest and the divine armour that protects as we pass through the doorway into that rest is another of the uncounted—and uncountable—blessings He has secured for us through His atonement and the covenant of peace He shares with us.[78]

Your senior pastor is not Jesus. Your bishop is not Jesus. Your company boss is not Jesus. This should be obvious and should go without saying but, unfortunately, in the twenty-first century, far too many Christian believers need to be told it again and again.

There is not a single person in authority over you who can be your spiritual covering. Only Jesus can.

Deep in our hearts, mostly hidden even from ourselves, there's an element of disappointment in the realisation that our covering has to be Jesus, and only Jesus. We crave a human protector, one we can see and touch, to defend us and battle for us, to stand up for us, to tell us what the right choice is, to blame when matters don't turn out the way we want. 'Give us a king,' the people of Israel said to the prophet Samuel.

> *And the Lord said to Samuel, 'Obey the voice of the people in all that they say to you, for they have not rejected you, but they have rejected Me from being king over them.'*
>
> 1 Samuel 8:7 ESV

God had told the people the terrible price of a human king, but they went ahead anyway. So it is that many today, even knowing the terrible price of having a king and a covering other than Jesus, still choose the flesh-and-blood option. To draw near to God—the deepest desire of the divine Lover for us—is too frightening. Just as the people said to Moses at Sinai that they wanted to have Moses relay God's words to them rather than have direct communication with Him, so today many people still want an intermediary.[79] We have a mediator, a perfect one—Jesus—but Covering Theology subtly proclaims He's not sufficient, He's not up to the task at hand and He needs the help of a set of human kings. Millions of people who would emphatically reject the doctrine of the infallibility of the pope nonetheless daily submit to a leader as if the concept was true at a local level, just not a universal one.

We don't need kings, we need judges—in the Othniel or Deborah sense of 'judge'.[80] Too many leaders who practice Covering Theology slide into *binding* as their form of *covering*—since binding and covering are, after all, basically both encompassed by the Hebrew word, 'lot'. It's such an easy transition that many leaders find it simple to justify and rationalise the shift to themselves. But 'lot' is one of the forms of covering with occult overtones.[81] It has a lingering sense of the dark arts of Egypt with its spiritual inversions that result in a defilement over our prayer life: we begin to consistently receive the opposite of what we pray for.[82]

> *On this mountain He will swallow up the shroud that enfolds all peoples, the sheet that covers all nations; He will swallow up death forever.*
>
> Isaiah 25:7–8 BSB

In the Hebrew, *the shroud that enfolds* is 'ha'lot ha'lot', meaning *the binding the binding*—a double binding.

We are promised that Jesus, through His atoning sacrifice, has consumed and destroyed all such death wrappings over us. Any notion of 'headship' pronounced by a leader that creates a buffer zone, an umbrella, a shield or any other euphemism for a covering is making the erroneous claim that the atonement of Jesus—that is, His covering of us—is in some way defective.

Considerable confusion exists about headship and covering. Most of the muddle results from various translations of 1 Corinthians 11:3. The English Standard Version is fairly representative:

> *I want you to understand that the head of every man is Christ,*
> *the head of a wife is her husband,*
> *and the head of Christ is God.*

Now by the time you've got to *'the head of Christ is God',* that vigilance I mentioned just a couple of paragraphs ago should have your mind darting to and fro, like a meerkat spotting a scorpion trying to creep past unnoticed. These words, *'the head of Christ is God,'* are straightforward heresy. They deny the co-equality of the Trinity. Therefore the translation *head* CANNOT be correct.

If we look for an alternative, one is readily available. Besides meaning *head*, the Greek word 'kephalé' also means *cornerstone*.

I want you to understand that the cornerstone of every man is Christ, the cornerstone of a wife is her husband, and the cornerstone of Christ is God.

This puts an entirely different complexion on the passage. It's not about superiority but about covenantal entryways and doors of reconciliation. Instead of *'the head of every man is Christ'*, it becomes 'the door of reconciliation for every man is Christ'. The sense of at_one_ment that nuances *cornerstone* means that 'the cornerstone of Christ is God' expresses covenantal unity between two Persons of the Trinity, rather than a heterodox hierarchy.

Furthermore, *cornerstone* with its sense of *head of the corner* fits perfectly with the rest of Paul's strange discourse about *covering*. The Hebrew word for *cornerstone* is derivative of *covering*, and—in what must have been an almost irresistible multilingual pun—Hebrew 'kaphar', *covering*, is just a lisp away from Greek 'kephalé', *head* or *cornerstone*. Paul's mysterious, almost bizarre, instruction that *'a wife should have a symbol of authority on her head* [cornerstone]*, because of the angels'* suddenly has context and sense.

Angels don't have anything much to do with *heads* but they have everything to do with *cornerstones*. In fact angels and cornerstones have been together since the beginning of creation, as God reveals to Job when He's questioning him:

> *'Where were you when I laid the foundation of the earth?*
>
> *Tell Me, if you have understanding...*
>
> *On what were its bases sunk?*
>
> *Or who laid its cornerstone,*
>
> *When the morning stars sang together*
>
> *And all the sons of God shouted for joy?'*
>
> Job 38:4,6-7 NASB

As things start out, so they progress. Whenever there's a threshold event in Scripture, there's an angel sentinel stationed watching over the cornerstone. These stones on the threshold can be anything from physical gateways to a new name—like Cephas, *cornerstone*, at Christ's inauguration of His church—to a step through the doorway of time from one year to the next, one season to the next, or one era to the next. If there's a threshold in Scripture, there's an angel—and often a pair of them—to go with it. Their job is to defend the portal and to check to make sure no one passes who is not able to show the right covenant authorisation. From their appearance barring the gateway back into Eden right on through to guarding the opening to heaven as Jesus ascended, their presence heralds the moment of change. Gabriel's messages about the birth of John the Baptiser and his cousin Jesus announce the entry of God into the world. Sometimes the change involves the closing of a door as when the Angel,

War, declared he was leaving the people to fend for themselves because of their disobedience.[83]

Thresholds, cornerstones and angels go together quite naturally. Paul's requirement that a woman should have a symbol of authority on her cornerstone *'because of the angels'* makes total sense while having one on her head or her husband is quite baffling.

Covering is not about someone in authority being our protector. It's about atonement, at_one_ment, reconciliation and covenant. It's about Jesus.

A cornerstone does not dictate or override conscience as a 'head' is apt to do, it sets the orientation for the house and household.[84]

A cornerstone does not dominate or control as a 'head' is apt to do, it's a place of welcome, of hospitality and honouring, reconciliation and rejoicing.

A cornerstone does not demand submission or subjection as a 'head' is apt to do, it's an altar where a covenant of mutual defence and sacrificial safeguarding is pledged.

If it sounds strange to equate cornerstones and people, remember Simon was called Cephas, *cornerstone*, though we tend to name him Peter *the rock*. And recall that we are *living stones*[85] with Christ as the *Chief* Cornerstone.

Jesus is the Chief Cornerstone, Chief Covenant Defender and Chief Kinsman-Redeemer. Though He may charge us to act as a cornerstone, a covenant defender or a kinsman-redeemer, it is as His agents and ambassadors, not as occupiers of His throne. Not as head, not as covering, but as covenant partners in advancing His kingdom in our generation and into the age to come.

Just as there's a *stone* word that is associated with *covering*—'keph'[86]—there's also a *stone* word related to *uncovering*. In truth, anyone who claims to 'cover' us by inserting themselves between us and Jesus is not simply a false covering, but someone who has in reality *uncovered* us. That *stone* word that denotes *uncovering* is 'gol' and it is connected to 'golah', *revealing secrets* and *exile*.

It's not just that a leader double binds us, it's that the inevitable result is *exile*. Invariably, those who proclaim themselves as a head, a covering, a source of blessing or protection will force anyone who is looking first and foremost to Jesus into exile one way or another. Even if we leave of our own accord in an attempt to escape the double bind, as we throw off the bindings and the coverings, we are uncovered—even if momentarily. That's the moment the spirit of wasting strikes with the 'gol' stone—we're hit like Goliath. His name, not coincidentally, means *the revealer of secrets, the exposer of nakedness, the one who exiles*. And his power was such that, even dead, he managed to be the cause of the exile of David.

How do we return from exile? Without an invitation, we can't.

Look around the world of Christendom today. There are far, far, far more exiles than there are prodigals. Most exiles continue to practise their faith quietly and in private—and often, in their isolation and loneliness, their experience of God is deeper, more intimate, drenched in glory. Yet because the trauma of the double-bind betrayal is compounded by the trauma of exile, then forty years later, they are still an outcast—because the double bind is still in operation, still defiling their lives.

They've lost their calling. They were stripped of their mantle. There is no way back.

Most damaged of all are their children who, as a result of the process of exile, have shaken off all belief in God. It's with that younger generation that the spirit of wasting triumphs so thoroughly—because impressionable children watch leaders proclaim bonds of love and family every Sunday but then fetter their parents in double bonds of abuse and sadism. Even if dad and mum don't say a word against those leaders—and they rarely do, since false loyalty is part of what empowers this situation—the children have seen and experienced the reality of exile. At the back of their minds from that point on is surely: why on earth would anyone put themselves through that, if that's what church, love and family is really all about? Better to stay away in the first place than suffer the pain of rejection and exile—*again*.

Exile is not the same as rejection. God calls us to master, to overcome, to prevail against the spirit of rejection. Yet, even when we succeed in that arena, it will not have any impact on exile. That is overturned by an invitation to return.

But more than an invitation is needed to bring our exile to an end.

So too is a recall. That is, a re-call: a reinstatement of calling. The initial calling was lost to the spirit of wasting through the double bind. The re-calling may be the same as the original, a complete restoration. Or more likely, it's a renovation, a renewal, a complete makeover.

This is the enormous wonder of the atonement: it is the provision of the One whose sacrifice is an all-sufficient covering even for the rebuilding of a calling that has been totally wrecked, an inheritance that has been utterly defiled and despoiled, a mantle that has been stolen and ruined.

In all the meanings of covering and uncovering that shape our lives, there is still one to consider. It's the one used by insurance brokers when they ask: how much *cover* do you want? As we look at the 'house' that represents our lives and the extreme devastation wrought by the whirlwind of impatience at one extreme and passivity at the other, by do-nothing on the one hand and double binds on the other, we'd be wise ask our ever-faithful paracletes, Jesus and the Holy Spirit, to come as insurance assessors. I imagine the Holy Spirit looking over our bombed-out ruins and saying, 'Can We cover this? Is there sufficient covering to fix this?'

And I imagine Jesus just smiling. And then I imagine this: at the time of the Last Judgment at the end of the age, Jesus will gather us up and escort us to the Father and with unalloyed delight He'll present us before the throne. And He'll say something like this: 'Recognise these guys, Abba? Surely You do. No? Three guesses! Give up?'

Yes, we should be unrecognisable. The atonement of Jesus should have so covered our restoration from ruin what we looked like before will be forgotten. We'll be unimaginably glorious. All that is false will be gone and we'll be overshadowed by His love. At that moment, Jesus should be able to shout in triumph before the Father, 'See! See! See! See what My blood has wrought! See what it has covered! It was all worth it.'

Jesus wants to uncover us in the fullness of time as a work of art restored to better than its original design. And His grace is brought to bear through the covering power of His blood to see our complete restoration through to its end. His atonement ushers in the salvation that angels long to look into. Through it, the manifold wisdom of God will be revealed to both the heavenly hosts and the authorities of darkness. All creation will have a wild celebration, shouting for joy just as the sons of God did when the cornerstone of the universe was first laid. Because the Cornerstone of the new heavens and the new earth has come and His blood and atoning sacrifice is enough to cover the mending of this entire broken world.

Prayers

Read through the following three prayers and, in consultation with the Holy Spirit, decide which one of them—if any—is right for you to speak out over your life.

1

Lord Jesus of Nazareth, Son of the Most High God,

I'm in the worst possible trouble. I'm in a double bind and there's no way out. No matter what I do, it will be wrong. I will dishonour myself, I will dishonour someone else and I will dishonour You. I've been set up for retaliation, false accusation, loss of provision, loss of inheritance, destruction of all the good I've achieved. I'm the chosen scapegoat; I've been silenced and muzzled and abused. I've been denied access to Your atonement by the double bind and no amount of faith, forgiveness or repentance is going to make any difference to that.

So I call on You for help. Please come into this situation with Your whip and overturn those who are trying to trade my life as the sacrifice for the maintenance of their own power and reputation. I know when You come with Your whip, chaos will erupt. Grant me Your peace in the midst of the chaos. Return to me access to Yourself and Your atonement and forbid retaliation against me for this prayer.

Grant me grace.

I ask this of the Father in Your name, as my Covenant Defender and Kinsman-Redeemer.

Amen

2

Lord Jesus of Nazareth,

You are the Resurrection and the Life. You are the Light of the World. You called Lazarus forth from the tomb and ordered, 'Unbind him and let him go.' Lord, please call me forth and declare the same on my behalf. I ask You to direct Your servants—human or angelic—to roll back the stone that is keeping me imprisoned in darkness and then to free me from the death wrappings that have been used to keep me immobile, silent, even unable to call for help.

Please also direct the death wrappings to be burnt so they can never be used against me or anyone else ever again. Please lift any defilement from me that they have left on me and surround me with the fragrance of Your victory over death. Grant me access to Yourself and also to Your atonement and forbid retaliation against me for this prayer.

I ask this of the Father in Your name, as my Covenant Defender and Kinsman-Redeemer.

Amen

3

Lord Jesus of Nazareth, my Covenant Defender and Kinsman-Redeemer,

Please grant me Your covenant of peace. I'm about to step up as a protector for someone in my family of faith and I realise I'm about to enter a curse. The person I'm about to confront has been angry without a cause and so has committed murder of the heart. There is defilement all around and, to atone for the murder of the heart, the anger of the person I'm about to confront needs to be slain. Please let it be slain by Love, be nailed to Your cross, to meet its end there.

You are asking me to be Your image-bearer as a covenant defender and kinsman-redeemer in this situation. Because of the curse, I ask Your kiss upon me and also upon the person whose innocence I am hoping to show. I ask for Your armour through that kiss and I ask that You will guard the heart of the one I am defending so that their faith is not shattered. Lord, let me know the moment before I start to step out of line so that I am not usurping Your position but always acting as Your ambassador. Give me the words to speak and tell me when to keep quiet. Do not allow me to be muzzled or gagged, silenced or suppressed. Let Your covenant of peace be over me, the one I'm protecting, the one I'm confronting. Give us all an understanding of Your perfect will for this situation.

Grant me access to Yourself, to Your presence and to Your atonement. Please forbid retaliation against me or my family, including my family of faith, for this prayer.

I ask this of Your Father and mine in Your name, as my Covenant Defender and Kinsman-Redeemer.

Amen

Prayer for the Children

Heavenly Father, I pray for my children and all the children of the world damaged by the double binding and spiritual exile their parents experienced.

Invite them back, Father, into Your presence. Send out invitations, day by day by day. Pursue them relentlessly and tell them repeatedly that exile is not Your will. Whisper to their hearts that Your love is waiting and that loneliness and displacement, isolation and separation are not of You. Issue both a call and a re-call, a reinstatement of all the inheritance that has been torn from them.

In Your grace, Father, stretch out the covering of the prayer shawl of Jesus so all of us—parents and children, leaders and followers—are sheltered, close to His heart, and bound only to Him by cords of love and joy, peace and patience, kindness and goodness, faithfulness and gentleness, Spirit-empowered self-control. May we know one another by such Fruit.

Remove any and all stones of uncovering and exile from our lives and replace them with the one and only Cornerstone that covers, reconciles and atones—Jesus of Nazareth. Thank You for the all-sufficiency of His atonement and its power to bring the exiles home.

In His name

Amen

Appendix 1

Summary

The spirit of wasting is one of seven threshold spirits. Like many of them, she goes by more than one name. Two of them are Rachab and Asherah.

When Python, the spirit of constriction, loosens its throttling grip on us, we often feel a sense of release and expansion. But this may simply be a temptation by Rachab to take on too much and so get burned out.

In the first instance, where we are dealing with wasting alone and not as part of a united cabal, we don't need to war to any significant degree against it. So long as we have overcome the spirit of rejection and put all known false refuges behind us, as well as revoked any covenants that we're aware of, then the Angel named War, also called God's Terror or His hornet, will drive out wasting ahead of us. We simply need to obey the angel's directions. We also need to have patience as the angel will move slowly in order to ensure that no power void is created and that we can hold the ground that has already been taken. We need to be careful to inquire of God before taking any steps that might bring us into covenant with those who are opposed to God and who will double bind us in the future.

PATIENCE is the weapon from the arsenal of the Fruit of the Spirit that is effective against wasting. But it needs supernatural wisdom in its deployment: too much patience is as problematic as too little. Both may put us back into the hands of the spirit of wasting.

When it is clear that we are close to overcoming all seven threshold spirits on an individual basis and that we are committed to God, for better or for worse, the spirit of wasting will form a coalition with all the others to try to ruin all that we've achieved to that point. Together, they will try to strip us of the inheritance we have begun to enjoy, steal the mantle we're just learning how to operate and snatch the divine assignment we've been given so that it lies abandoned and unfinished. Their main strategy to pull off this campaign is to find someone in authority over us or someone to whom we are willing to cede power over us [called the 'leader' for shorthand throughout this book, although they may not normally be so] who is capable of putting us in a double bind.

A double bind is designed to deprive us of access to the atonement of Jesus and thus to the power that activates every aspect of our calling.

There are three options for removal of a double bind (other than simply resigning from whatever position we're in that gives the other person power over us) and they are:

- Invite Jesus to come into the situation with a whip
- Ask Jesus to command that the death wrappings on us are removed, destroyed and any defilement lifted
- Ask for a covenant of peace if it is necessary to enter a curse

Since these are mostly violent solutions, then in each case, it's wise to pray to the Father to forbid retaliation. Ask for access to the atonement to be restored not just for ourselves but for anyone involved in the wider situation.

Jesus, as the Chief Cornerstone, is the one who perfectly atones and reconciles. There is also a counterfeit of this stone that does the opposite: it exiles instead of reconciles. Instead of covering, it uncovers. Instead of blessing and protecting, it defiles and destroys.

Any claim by a leader to cover us is false and is actually an attempt to uncover us by usurping the position of Jesus in our lives. To agree to their covering is to allow them to assume the throne of God in our lives. (The term 'covering' here does not, of course, refer to acts like 'prayer covering' or a leader's general defence of our character or standing up on our behalf; it refers to a theological understanding that it is necessary to be completely submissive to a leader, right or wrong, in order not to come under a curse.) We should never offer a human being the kind of trust that rightfully belongs only to God. Sooner or later, we will find ourselves in a position where the choice is to submit to God or to the leader. The spirit of wasting will take the opportunity to tie a double bind into the situation. Dishonour, abuse and exile will be the most likely results. Loyalty to God does not guarantee that severe trauma will not be experienced.

Appendix 2

Glossary of Selected Terms

Anat	a berserker war-goddess of the ancient Canaanites; a deity who claimed to have conquered every major spirit including Death and maintained the right to confer kingship amongst the principalities of the nations. Jesus warred against her at Cana, Sychar and in the garden after the resurrection. She is a spirit of dispossession and disinheritance and claims to sovereignty of appointed time. Another name for this spirit is Lilith.
Asherah	a fertility goddess of the ancient Canaanites; the mother of the seventy young lions who were the principalities ruling the nations. Jesus warred against her when He walked on water. She is often symbolised by a tree or a pole. She is a spirit of

wasting. Another name for this spirit is Rachab.

Azazel — the demon goat-god to whom God commanded that a scapegoat bearing the sins of the people be sent on the Day of Atonement. In Jewish tradition, Azazel was one of the main leaders of the Watcher-angels who descended to Mount Hermon with the purpose of seeking mates amongst human women. Jesus warred against him at Caesarea Philippi and during the Transfiguration. Another name for this spirit of rejection and panic is Pan.

Belial — a demonic entity who was considered the chief of the sons of darkness in Jewish tradition. The defilement of Belial on people and places is so great that God commanded whole cities to be destroyed and never rebuilt, as well as all the people killed. He is a spirit of abuse and armies. Although 'Belial' is used as a personal name for a fallen angel 28 times in Scripture, it is usually hidden 27 of those times under the descriptor 'worthless'. Another name for this spirit is Kronos.

Cornerstone the first stone laid for the foundation of a building, it was placed where the doorway was intended to go and thus set the orientation of the building. It had a shallow basin carved into it to catch blood dripping from the lintels and doorposts. This blood would not only be painted there at the Passover but at any time a guest was due to arrive. It was a symbol of hospitality. The cornerstone was also an altar and a place where covenant was ratified. A guest who 'passed over' the blood covenanted with the host. A guest who stumbled, struck the stone, dashed their foot, or trampled on the blood refused covenant.

According to the traditions of Freemasonry, the orientation of the Tabernacle in the wilderness was set by Moses using two thin poles called 'asherah'. Thus in Freemasonry ritual, the deacons still carry wands with a significance originating in these 'asherah'. As the tools that allegedly set the orientation and also mark the beginning for the erection of the Tabernacle, the 'asherah' of Freemasonry counterfeit the cornerstone.

Covenant of Peace	an agreement of oneness with God as Covenant Defender that offers protection for entering a curse as a covenant defender.
Covenant with Death	an agreement of oneness with Death that trades inheritance for survival. Not a death wish.
Covenant with Sheol	an agreement of oneness with the grave that trades prophetic sight or the gift of a seer in exchange for information. Not a death wish.
Defilement	moral uncleanness or spiritual pollution that can be transferred from a person, object or land to another.
False refuge	a first port-of-call habit for consolation during distress that is other than God.
Kronos	an elder-god of time (but *not* appointed time) who is also a spirit of abuse.
Leviathan	a sea monster created by God to frolic in the deep. In a spiritual sense, a courtier of God occupying the same space in the heavenly Temple as the Levites did in the earthly one. Leviathan is a spirit of retaliation who is on the lookout for dishonour and disrespect. He is king of the sons of pride.

Lilith	a vampiric spirit who is particularly focused on draining our resurrection life. Her other face is Anat.
Name Covenant	an agreement of oneness with another person (including God) in which an exchange of names is involved. It differs from a blood covenant in that it is about friendship, rather than family.
Python	the spirit of constriction who tries to pressure us into an unloving choice or an ungodly sacrifice. Its occult speciality is divination.
Rachab	a sea monster. In the spiritual sense, the spirit of wasting. Her other name is Asherah.
Salt Covenant	an agreement of oneness that involves eating together and consuming food seasoned with salt. Salt is a symbol of permanency.
Threshold	place where a cornerstone has been laid.
Threshold Covenant	a covenant ratified by 'passing over' a cornerstone. It involves hospitality and protection and implies vows of mutual defence. When a host raises a threshold covenant with a guest, the pair become covenant defenders

of one another and are expected to expend their strength, to the death, if an attack occurs. Normally this covenant is temporary—just during the visit of the guest—but a salt covenant makes it permanent.

Threshold Guardians	angelic authorities who watch over thresholds to allow or disbar entry. Although the term 'threshold guardians' in this series is usually used in a negative sense for fallen angels, most angels who appear in Scripture are holy and are present at a transition period in history to guard the door into the new era. Also called throne guardians from their original office as courtiers of God's throne room.
Ziz	the spirit of forgetting or of tearing truth apart. Often called 'Jezebel' though strictly Jezebel is the name for a person, not a spirit. Quite often Ziz is the threshold spirit that most people first encounter though, because Ziz is so efficient at making us forget, we are unlikely to remember any conflict with her.

Endnotes

1. It's a 96% failure rate in the first ten years. That is 24 out of 25 businesses do not last a decade.

2. In fact, I've undoubtedly added to the confusion because the spelling I use is the reverse of the spelling most academics use. My apologies.

3. 'Do-Nothing' is the NIV translation. JB Phillips, one of my favourite translators, renders this verse, *'That is why I call her [Egypt] the Spent Whirlwind,'* thereby indicating this fallen spirit is one of the cherubim, since they can manifest as whirlwinds. The RSV gives it as: *'Therefore have I called her Rahab who sits still.'* Egypt is depicted as full of blustering, braggart speech, promising much but fulfilling nothing. See: biblehub.com/sermons/isaiah/30-7.htm (accessed 30 December 2024)

4. Procrastination is being touted relentlessly at the moment as a depression response. In my view, it's more of an avoidance-of-conflict response, though ultimately it tends to provoke more conflict than it avoids.

5. *The Elijah Tapestry—John 1 and 21: Mystery, Majesty and Mathematics in John's Gospel #1;*

   Dealing with Lilith: Spirit of Dispossession: Strategies for the Threshold #10;

   In the Meshes of the Net: Jesus and the Healing of History #06;

   Dealing with Kronos: Spirit of Abuse and Time: Strategies for the Threshold #9.

6   The echoes of the past I am referring to here involve recapitulation as distinct from typology. Biblical typology is a symbolic way of looking at actions and events in the Hebrew Scriptures and seeing in them a prophetic foreshadowing of the coming of Jesus. The reason I prefer recapitulation to typology is because recapitulation offers the possibility of a divergence from the old, original storyline.

7   We could look at this scene in terms of typology or of recapitulation. Typology refers to historical people, places, objects, or events which foreshadow Christ and His work. Typologically speaking, Elijah's angelic breakfast foreshadows the breakfast Jesus baked for His disciples and His interaction with Peter. But from the perspective of recapitulation, this is the fork in the road between the two stories. Elijah did not turn back to his calling, but Peter did. In fact, Peter is tasked by Jesus with completing the assignment originally given to Elijah that had been waiting more than eight centuries for fulfillment. And that task was the ingathering of the Gentiles.

8   There are two likely locations for Ramoth Gilead, the fortress where Jehu was stationed. One is a mere five kilometres (three miles) from Tishbe, Elijah's hometown. The other is about thirty kilometres away.

9   See: *The Elijah Tapestry—John 1 and 21: Mystery, Majesty and Mathematics in John's Gospel #1*.

10 In the language of Ugarit, the construction b+Sr+h (preposition + noun + suffix) connected to Asherah refers to making something that is woven. The noun, Sr, could refer to a *prince, song, navel, torch, line* or *evil*. She is the mother of seventy princes, her name sounds like the Hebrew for *I will sing*.

11 We can safely assume she was the main deity Jezebel summoned because she would have been one of

Jezebel's patrons. Jezebel's name means 'Where is the prince?' and comes from a ritual shout to summon Baal-Hadad from the underworld at the end of winter. The words originated in the repeated cry of Anat as she sought Baal-Hadad after she'd buried him and then went looking for him. (An unusual sequence that is paralleled by the actions of Mary the Magdalene as, together, she and Jesus completely despoil every aspect of Canaanite religion as it pertains to Anat and Baal-Hadad. See: *The Summoning of Time—John 2 and 20: Mystery, Majesty and Mathematics in John's Gospel #2*) Another reason we can assume Jezebel's patron was Anat is because her daughter, Athaliah, who became queen of Judah, is named after Anat.

12 Ben-hadad the king is not the same as Baal-Hadad, the storm-god.

13 The delay could have been as much as two decades.

14 Jonah 3:4 NKJV

15 The story of the destruction of Jabesh Gilead is told *after* the story of Jephthah in the Book of Judges. It's part of the saga of the civil war between the clans of Benjamin and all the other tribes of Israel. Although it appears to be out of sequence, the Book of Judges is only mostly, not entirely, chronological. Instead the stories are ordered according to the increasing severity of threshold covenant violation. Since Phinehas appears as high priest during the civil war, the destruction of Jabesh Gilead occurred well before the close of the era of the Judges and thus before Jephthah's time.

16 Jim Wilder & Ray Woolridge, *Escaping Enemy Mode: How Our Brains Unite or Divide Us*, Moody Press 2022

17 See: *God's Panoply: The Armour of God and the Kiss of Heaven*, Armour Books 2013

18 Emphasis mine

19 The word 'nachash' for *serpent* also means *enchantment*.

20 David is also passive in other circumstances involving abuse. He doesn't support Mephibosheth, the son of Jonathan, against Ziba, Mephibosheth's servant. He initially believes Ziba's claim that Mephibosheth is opportunistically waiting to be made king and so he gives Mephibosheth's inheritance to Ziba. When he discovers Ziba has lied, he does not reverse his decision but tells Mephibosheth to sort it out himself. As if a lame man with one young son can contend with an able-bodied and manipulative man with twelve sons. With this action, David effectively dispossessed the last remaining member of the House of Saul. It may not have been revenge but the optics aren't good. It certainly gives the impression that David is repeatedly complicit with the spirit of abuse through indifference and passive cruelty.

21 Emphases mine

22 Elijah's mantle passes to Elisha, then to Elisha's protégé, Jonah, then to John the Baptiser, then through the hands of Jesus to Simon Peter. Older translations of John 21:15, such as the King James Version, in the post-resurrection scene where Jesus is restoring Peter, read, 'Simon, son of Jonah,' while more modern translations are 'Simon, son of John'. If it's unclear whether Peter is son of Jonah or son of John, then perhaps John the Baptiser might have been Jonah the Baptiser—and thus the angel's announcement of his name was to indicate he carried the mantle of the prophet Jonah.

23 Maybe he was waiting to see if she was pregnant before meting out any punishment to Amnon. It's a callous reaction but in keeping with David's responses

in other situations. If this were the case, apparently by the time he was sure, his procrastination was already so long it was easier to continue to do nothing than to take action.

24 Though, having said that, sometimes none of those work either. The atonement is a matter of grace but we can come to believe it is a matter of transaction: that in exchange for more faith, more repentance, more forgiveness, more declarations of the Word of God, more prophetic decrees, then God will break through for us in the way we need. All of these things are simply trying to add to the atonement of Jesus; they effectively imply it was not enough. Worse still, sometimes we are in the position of trying to buy grace. See: *Hidden in the Cleft: True and False Refuge: Strategies for the Threshold #4*, Armour Books 2020

25 Matthew 18:19

26 Genesis 15:12

27 See: the third book in this series, *Name Covenant: Invitation to Friendship: Strategies for the Threshold #3*, Armour Books 2018

28 See: *God's Pageantry: The Threshold Guardians and the Covenant Defender*, Armour Books 2015

29 The ancient Greek word for *hospitality* was 'philoxenia', *friendship of strangers*.

30 See: faithrethink.com/7-atonement-theories-from-church-history/ (accessed 27 December 2024) for an explanation of these different theories.

31 There's no real need for a satanic covenant to have a faithfulness clause. If you're loyal to the satan, he's got you. If you're disloyal to him, you're breaking covenant and therefore curses rain down on you. He's still got you.

32 See: *Hidden in the Cleft: True and False Refuge: Strategies for the Threshold #4*, Armour Books 2020

33 See: *God's Panoply: The Armour of God and the Kiss of Heaven*, Armour Books 2016

34 That book was *God's Panoply: The Armour of God and the Kiss of Heaven*. I'd been arguing with God for several years about starting it, telling Him repeatedly He'd chosen the wrong person to write it. At last, He convinced me differently.

35 A 'catch-22' is a paradoxical situation where there is no possibility of escape. The trapped individual has no avenue of breakthrough or of getting away because of contradictory rules or limitations put in place by an authority who refuses to change any of the rules to remove the internal conflict. The name comes from Joseph Heller's novel, *Catch-22*, which describes intolerable psychological control involving combat missions during World War II: if you're not worried about a mission, then you fly; but if you are worried about a mission, this is a rational fear, so you still fly. There's no way to prove you're dangerously traumatised, so either way, you must fly. Catch-22s often result from rules, regulations, or procedures that an individual is subject to, but has no control over, because to fight the rule is to accept it. As Wikipedia says, 'One connotation of the term is that the creators of the "catch-22" situation have created arbitrary rules in order to justify and conceal their own abuse of power.'

36 The terminology of 'power encounter' and 'truth encounter' comes from Arthur Burk. A power encounter is a confrontation with spiritual darkness that relies for success on the authority and righteousness of the person conducting the deliverance session. A truth encounter, on the other hand, has come to be the most common form of healing and deliverance, involving confession, repentance, forgiveness, renunciation and the application of the Cross. The minister can be the most unrighteous person on the face of the earth and a truth encounter will still be transformational because it has nothing to do with the minister, it has to do with Jesus and the Cross.

37 Consonance is a poetic term, not an etymological one. The repeated testimony of Scripture is that God is a poet, a wordsmith, and that humanity is, as Ephesians 2:10 says in the Greek 'His poetry'. Name covenants and prophetic declarations of destiny use poetry more often than they use word etymology. Therefore, in my view, it's wise to explore consonance, assonance, rhyme, alliteration and other lyric forms when it comes to understanding the meaning of a word.

38 2 Timothy 3:8

39 He violated the commandment outlined in Exodus 30:11–16.

40 Matthew 23:33 NASB

41 The Hebrew word for *trade* in this case indicates bartering in both names and reputations. It also implies *gossiping*.

42 See: *Dealing with Leviathan: Spirit of Retaliation: Strategies for the Threshold #5*, Armour Books 2020

43 Twice in Isaiah 27:1.

44 I'm using 'detective' in its most ancient sense here—that of someone who uncovers a roof to peer down inside and find what is concealed.

45 *Covering Theology* is very similar to the Shepherding or Discipleship Movement that was prevalent in charismatic circles in the late twentieth century. It is now commonly taught in Pentecostal circles as well and is increasingly prevalent in evangelical circles and beyond. Those five respected leaders who founded the Shepherding movement either dissociated themselves from it (Derek Prince) or publicly repented of it (Bob Mumford) when they saw the abuses that arose because of their teaching. Similar extreme abuse occurs with Covering Theology. Some of its tenets are:

- All authority is instituted by God.
- The five-fold ministry (apostles, prophets, evangelists, pastors and teachers) is God's authority on earth.
- Obedience to the Lord requires obedience to God's delegated authority, even if they are wrong.
- Rebellion against God's delegated authority is rebellion against God.
- Blessing comes to those who suffer under authority while rebellion against authority opens a person to curses and the demonic realm.
- God does not judge people on the fruit of their life but on how faithfully they followed authority.

There are other principles as well (see: coveringandauthority.com/covering-theology-101/—accessed 31 December 2024 or Allan Clare, *Damaged by God: A Critical Analysis of 'Covering Theology' with Particular Reference to John Bevere's 'Under Cover',* 2012.)

46 See: thegospelcoalition.org/themelios/article/failure-to-atone-rethinking-davids-census-in-light-of-exodus-30/ (accessed 20 November 2024)

47 1 Chronicles 21:6 This story shows how complex a personality Joab was. Up to this point, he appears completely ruthless and utterly insensitive to the spiritual world. But throughout this episode he is much more in tune with God than David was.

48 Mark Wolynn, *It Didn't Start with You: How Inherited Family Trauma Shapes Who We Are and How to End the Cycle*, Penguin 2016

49 1 Corinthians 12:27–1 Corinthians 13:13

50 1 Chronicles 16:22 KJV and Psalm 105:15 KJV

51 Conviction is not the same as condemnation. The conviction of the Holy Spirit is a warning sense of 'don't do that' along with a need for repentance as a remedy, whereas condemnation is a sense of shame where the only remedy is to bury the humiliation alive and try to forget it, instead of reconciling with God.

52 Rather it is a title of the Godhead that goes back to the very beginning of creation when the Spirit moved across the face of the waters. Furthermore, even in terms of ships, the title is also God's to claim since He was the one who set the ark of Noah 'walking' on the water.

53 Perhaps even the apostle Paul stepped across the line of demarcation mentioned by Jude that, in dealing with high level angelic powers, we should restrict ourselves to 'The Lord rebuke you.' It certainly didn't go well for his ministry in Philippi after he exorcised Python. He himself was evicted from town by the time 24 hours were up. Note that he cast out the spirit, then he was cast out.

54 See: cambridge.org/core/journals/new-testament-studies/article/abs/ancient-binding-spells-amulets-and-matt-161819-revisiting-august-dells-proposal-a-century-later/C6BCE92DD0E52CFD5B8871458D67ED78 (accessed 30 November 2024)

55 John 12:48. See: Derek Prince, *Judging: When? Why? How?*, Whitaker House 2001

56 Symphony is the word that Jesus uses in Matthew 18:19 to describe *being in agreement* in prayer.

57 The word 'tiqveh' is derived from 'qavah', *wait, collect, line, measure, bind, gather, be patient*.

58 Deuteronomy 16:21

59 The iconography of ibexes associated with Asherah is also associated with Tanit, the patron of ancient Carthage. Tanit was the consort of Baal-Hammon, a goddess of war, a mother goddess and a nurse. Those functions align more closely with Anat than with Asherah—though, over time, many of the goddesses of antiquity came to be a fusion of two or more.

60 Sometimes the title 'Mistress of Animals' is attributed to the Canaanite goddess Anat, the daughter of Asherah. I have spiritually identified Anat with Lilith in *Dealing with Lilith: Spirit of Dispossession*, although no ancient literature associates them.

61 See: Karel van der Toorn, Bob Becking, Pieter Willem van der Horst, *Dictionary Of Deities And Demons In The Bible*, Wm. B. Eerdmans Publishing, 1999

62 The kings of the earth are symbolised as mountains.

63 1 Corinthians 6:3

64 Perhaps its central location as a Levitical city was instrumental in choosing it as the new site of the Tabernacle when the sanctuary at Shiloh diminished in importance. Shiloh's decline happened due to the loss of the Ark of the Covenant and the all-but-complete fall of the House of Eli. In addition, the fact that the designated Tabernacle servants, the hewers of wood and drawers of water, the Gibeonites, lived there would have factored in choosing it.

65 Jeremiah 17:9

66 This situation appears to have happened amongst the forebears of Jesus. The genealogy of Jesus as reckoned through Joseph is given in the first chapter of Matthew and the third chapter of Luke. Some scholars have attempted to remove the discrepancies by suggesting that one genealogy is really that of Mary, though both are stated to be reckoned through Joseph. However, the accounts can be reconciled if Joseph's grandfather Mattan (or Matthat) was born of a Levirate marriage. One genealogy then traces his biological line while the other genealogy traces the line imputed to him as a result of the kinsman-redeemer relationship. Either way, Joseph was descended from David.

67 Although Eli's genealogy is not given, this can be deduced because Ahimelech belonged to the House of Ithamar (1 Chronicles 24:3). Ahimelech was descended from Ahitub, (1 Samuel 22:20) who was descended from Eli. Therefore Eli must have been of the House of Ithamar. Ithamar was a son of Aaron. His name means *land of palms*. One of Asherah's most notable symbols was the palm.

68 A tradition developed over the centuries that the priest 'anointed for war' would be the War Messiah, separate to the Royal Messiah and the Priestly Messiah. The War Messiah would allegedly come from the tribe of Ephraim and thus be called 'Son of Joseph', since Ephraim was Joseph's son, while the Priestly Messiah would be of the order of Melchizedek. Now it's quite peculiar to suggest that the War Messiah should be a priest but NOT a Levite of the line of Aaron. By the time of the first century, this expectation of several messiahs as well as their forerunner herald, the Elijah-who-was-to-come, had developed out of an interpretation of the Four Craftsmen mentioned in the prophecy of Zechariah 1:20.

69 Numbers 31:6

70 Psalm 85:10–11

71 If the leading proponents of Covering Theology truly believed it, then they would all repent for the Reformation since that was a supreme example of disobedience to ecclesiastical authority. Paul would have been sinning in opposing Peter and calling him out publicly. Since all authority has been created by God, the 'exousias', the *authorities* I have repeatedly called *threshold spirits, threshold guardians* or *throne guardians*, have been created by Him too. Are we then to submit to these fallen cherubim and seraphim because they are authorities? Of course not! Are we to submit to those leaders who have fallen into one of these spirits' traps and have decided to double bind us? Covering Theology suggests we are blessed for doing so and for quietly suffering under such a yoke. Are we not to warn the leaders of their peril when they choose the 'exousias' rather than Jesus?

The assumption behind Covering Theology is that the delegated authority in the leadership of the church is somehow miraculously preserved from stepping outside God's Word or the will of the Holy Spirit. This is perilously similar to the doctrine of papal infallibility. If even Peter had to be brought back into line by Paul, what makes any leader think they are immune to error? The notion of *submission* as unquestioning obedience in Covering Theology is based in large measure on Romans 13:1;5. This understanding of 'hupotassó', the Greek word for *submission* is, in my view, entirely flawed. A comparison of Romans 13:1–12 (beginning with *'submit to the governing authorities'* and ending with *'put on the armour of light'*) with Ephesians 5:21–6:11 (beginning with *'submit to one another'* and ending with *'put on the armour of God'*) reveals a strong set of parallel thoughts based on the Hebrew concept of the *armour-bearer* or the Greek idea of the *paraclete*.

These parallels are detailed in *God's Panoply: The Armour of God and the Kiss of Heaven*. The Hebrew concept of *submission* is diametrically opposed to the Greek concept and, although Paul went to careful lengths to clarify that, we have isolated particular verses and so we have lost his original meaning.

72 We can take the sin of others onto ourselves like a scapegoat by the ancient practice of 'sin-eating' or 'disease-eating'. We may inappropriately burden-bear on behalf of others by taking on their grief or stress or sickness. There is legitimate burden-bearing, but we can go too far and take on the role of Christ and being the mediator or saviour and not allowing Him to take His rightful place in the life of the other person.

73 The Jewish people have long understood that the commitment between God and His people ratified at Mount Sinai was a marriage covenant and that what took place there was a wedding. See: jewish.org/library/article_cdo/aid/3676643/Jewish/Meditation-on-an-Embrace.htm (accessed 1 January 2025)

74 Numbers 31:8

75 William Albright suggested that Asherah's epithet, 'the one who treads the sea', is an abbreviation for 'the one who treads the sea-dragon'. Like Baal-Hadad, who claims to ride the clouds, she claims to walk on water or on a sea-monster. That sea-monster may be Rachab or it may be Leviathan or it may simply be a 'tanniyn', one of the great sea beings. If it's Rachab, then Asherah can also be identified with the dragon that she treads.

76 Deuteronomy 32:8. Some translations have *sons of Israel* instead of *sons of God*. This, however, is a result of a change about a thousand years ago in the Masoretic text. Some scribe in the tenth century or thereabouts decided to change the wording because dividing the nations among the angels was theologically uncomfortable. Older Hebrew manuscripts retain the

original wording. The number of nations remains the same, regardless of whether the wording is rendered as *sons of Israel* or as *sons of God*, but the entire worldview where principalities were given rulership of the nations was eliminated. See the works of Michael Heiser for a detailed explanation of the older worldview—God gave seventy angels guardianship and rulership of the nations while reserving the land of Israel for Himself and giving it to a people descended from a man and a woman He called into it from Ur of the Chaldees—Abram and Sarai.

77 The Israelites had been snared in a conspiracy and were in a double-bind. A league of four cities in the Gibeonite confederacy had devised a plan to maximise the chances of their own survival in the coming war. They covenanted with the people of Israel, thus trapping them in a spiritual dilemma. Whatever they did, the Israelites would be going against God. If they didn't go raze the Gibeonite cities, then they would disobey God's instructions to remove the people of the land. On the other hand, if they broke the covenant they'd just cut, that would be heinous since, as image-bearers of God, one of the most significant ways we can carry His name is by loyally upholding any covenants we have taken out. He is a covenant-keeping God. That is His essential nature.

78 There are four times, other than Numbers 25:12, where a *covenant of peace* is mentioned. These are Isaiah 54:10, Ezekiel 37:26, Ezekiel 34:25 and Malachi 2:5. The first two of these are promises that are very general in nature but the last two involve warnings regarding abuses by leaders, including the priesthood. By causing others to stumble (a word often associated with *dashing a foot against a cornerstone* and thereby repudiating an offer of covenant), the leaders have not only dishonoured God but, as a consequence, they will be cursed and so will their blessings. That is, the words of favour they speak over others will bring evil instead.

79 Exodus 20:18–19

80 Othniel was the first of the judges—the deliverers or champions—of Israel, who led portions of the nation prior to the advent of the kings. Deborah was the only female judge.

81 Another Hebrew word meaning *covering* is 'nasak' and it likewise has both holy and unholy connotations. It is related to 'nacak' which can mean *anoint a king* and *a drink offering*, but can also refer to the *molten image of an idol*. Similar to it is 'cakak', *cover, hedge, protect* or *overshadow*, a word that on the one hand describes the cherubim who *cover* the mercy seat but on the other is also used for the *covering* cherub who rebelled against God and was cast out of Eden for the violence of his trading. (Ezekiel 28:14;16)

82 For further details on Egyptian spiritualism, see: *Dealing with Lilith: Spirit of Dispossession: Strategies for the Threshold #10*, Armour Books 2024

83 Judges 2:1–5

84 As the first stone laid for the foundation, the way it is set determines the positioning of the doorway which, in ancient Hebrew dwellings, was in the corner, hence the name *cornerstone*. This threshold therefore oriented the rest of the house.

85 1 Peter 2:5

86 The word 'keph' is the origin of Cephas, the name Jesus gave to Simon and that we usually translate in its Greek form 'petros' for Peter, *rock*. Strictly speaking, Cephas (and therefore Peter) is better translated *cornerstone* as it is related to 'kapporeth', *mercy seat*, as well as 'kaphar', *cover, atone, reconcile,* or *purge*.

Dealing with Python:
Spirit of Constriction

Strategies for the Threshold #1

with Arpana Dev Sangamitrha

On the threshold into your unique calling in life a dark spiritual sentinel waits. Scripture names it 'Python'—it has a God-given right to be there and test your significant choices. Trying to cast it out of a situation is useless.

Paul encountered it just as the Gospel was transitioning across a major threshold: the watershed moment when Christianity moved from Asia to Europe.

This book explores the tactics of Python, as well as its agenda. It offers insight into what this spirit hopes to get out of you and how you can rectify past mistakes involving this constricting, cunning enemy.

Dealing with Ziz:
Spirit of Forgetting

Strategies for the Threshold #2

The most significant threshold point of life is the doorway into God's unique calling for us. He invites us through covenant to fulfil the destiny we were born to achieve.

However, many of us fall at the threshold, rather than pass over it. We experience constriction, wasting, retaliation and forgetting—to such a degree it's easy to doubt the promises of God.

Dealing with Ziz examines the spiritual implications of forgetting in relation to threshold covenants. Since the opposite of remembering is dismembering—dismembering of truth—the spirit of forgetting is able to block access to our calling.

Yet there is an answer, a Fruit of the Spirit that overcomes Ziz.

Name Covenant:

Invitation to Friendship

Strategies for the Threshold #3

Abram became Abraham. Jacob became Israel. Simon beame Peter.

Name covenanting seems at first like an archaic, long-discarded practice that disappeared in the first century around the time Saul became Paul. The patriarchs and apostles exchanged names and so received new destinies. But that was then. And this is now.

However name covenanting never went away.

Robert Louis Stevenson became Teriitera. Paul Gauguin became Tioka. James Cook became Terreeoboo. Arthur Phillip became Woollarwarre.

These recent examples throw light on this ancient practice of friendship and kinship. They show us that, when God offers a new name, more than simply a new calling is attached. It's an invitation to friendship with Him.

If you're wondering how to overcome the issues of the threshold and the associated ungodly covenants, this book has the answer. Other books help you recognise the problem, this one points out the first step on the path.

Hidden in the Cleft:
True and False Refuge

Strategies for the Threshold #4

Jesus had a refuge—a safe haven—He retreated to when His life was in danger.

What does His choice reveal about where best to find sanctuary in times of trouble? What is the significance of the hiding place He used for an entire season? How can we discern the difference between a true and false refuge?

Removal of our false refuges is the first step towards achieving our life's calling—the divine purpose for which God created us. Yet all too often we fail to recognise how we've defaulted to a false refuge when disappointment strikes.

This book offers practical help, hope and encouragement towards achieving your destiny in Christ.

Dealing with Leviathan:

Spirit of Retaliation

Strategies for the Threshold #5

Retaliation, reprisal, retribution—many of us express the ferocity of our encounters with the spirit of Leviathan with such words. Most believers are stunned by savagery of the backlash they experience, and are baffled by God's seeming failure to intervene.

Reparation, recompense, restitution, restoration—these promised corrections to injustice are smashed just as they seem within reach. Why does this happen?

As we examine Scripture, we find that Leviathan is an officer of God's royal court. When we violate the consecration of that Holy Place, it has the legal right to remove us. It does not do so gently.

Dealing with Leviathan offers insight into overcoming this spirit of the deep.

Dealing with Resheph:
Spirit of Trouble

Strategies for the Threshold #6

with Irenie Senior

Resheph is mentioned seven times in Scripture. A fallen seraph and throne guardian, it is identified here as a hidden face of Leviathan, the spirit that counterattacks against dishonour. Symbolised as a stag and an archer, Resheph is connected with flames and fire, fever, financial distress, mental illness, drought and scorching heat as well as the underworld.

Jesus warred against this spirit at least seven times. It's easy to miss these battles because it's easy to miss the prophecies Jesus was fulfilling and the mention of Resheph associated with them.

This is a companion volume to *Dealing With Leviathan* and examines the obstacles we face on the threshold into our calling.

Dealing with Azazel:

Spirit of Rejection

Strategies for the Threshold #7

'I am your only friend.'

That's the playbook line that works so superbly for the spirit of rejection. Most of us fall for it without ever realising our coping mechanisms—fight, flight, freeze, flatter, forestall or forget—are actually undermining our every effort to overcome this entity. So how can we subdue the spirit of rejection in our lives without sabotaging ourselves in the process?

This seventh book in the series, *Strategies for the Threshold*, addresses the nature of the spirit, its wider agenda, its spiritual legal rights, and its propensity for following after us to undo the good that we do.

Dealing with Belial:
Spirit of Armies and Abuse

Strategies for the Threshold #8

with Janice Speirs

'What harmony,' Paul asked, *'is there between Christ and Belial?'*

Where, you might wonder, did he pluck that name from? In most English Bibles, it appears for the first time in Paul's second letter to the Corinthians. So it comes as a surprise to realise this army commander of the spirit world is mentioned 27 times in Hebrew, almost always in connection with abuse and violence. Modern translations generally substitute *worthless.* Yet from the stories where Belial appears, we can draw important principles for dealing with its tactics, agenda and ploys.

This eighth book in the series, *Strategies for the Threshold*, examines the spiritual dynamics involved in approaching your life's calling.

Dealing with Kronos:
Spirit of Abuse and Time

Strategies for the Threshold #9

with Janice Speirs

The oldest stories about 'Father Time' describe an entity with a seraph's body, and heads like the angelic cherubim. Kronos is a voracious spirit of abuse who consumes the past. Bound in chains to prevent him eating the future, nevertheless through the power of unresolved past trauma he wants to devour the present too.

We can believe we've escaped abuse when, in reality, complicity with Kronos has locked us into a maximum security spiritual prison. We need the Redeemer of wasted time to aid us. Scripture provides unexpected and important principles for dealing with the tactics, agenda and ploys of Kronos.

This book is a companion volume to *Dealing with Belial*.

Dealing with Lilith:
Spirit of Dispossession

Strategies for the Threshold #10

Lilith is a threshold guardian with many aliases, including the war-monger goddess Anat of Zaphon. She is a vampiric spirit who specialises in dispossession and necromancy. She also claims rulership of appointed times as well as dwelling rights within us. By blocking the processing of shame, she tempts us towards narcissism or addiction.

The conflict between her and Jesus began at Cana and went on even after His return from the dead. Many prophets surrendered the fullness of their calling to her and only a very few triumphed over her.

Dealing With Lilith examines the work of Jesus in removing her spears, harpoons and entangling nets to restore our lost inheritance.

Core Values: Love

The DNA of God #1

with Rebekah Robinson

Taste and see that the Lord is good!

Galatians 5 describes the growing DNA of God in our lives as a list of attributes, or *fruit*, emanating from the Holy Spirit.

This first volume explores the love aspect of God's nature, and its outworking in the hearts of believers respective to His other flavours.

Core Values: Joy

The DNA of God #2

with Rebekah Robinson

The Kingdom of God is a matter of righteousness, peace, and joy in the Holy Spirit. This is a direct reflection of the nature of its King!

This second volume looks into the joy of the Lord, and how His joy overflows into our lives.

Core Values: Peace

The DNA of God #3

with Rebekah Robinson

The peace of God is said to 'pass all understanding.' What might it be like for the Lord to *be* peace? What could that mean for those of us who have invited Him to live entwined with us?

This third volume of the series explores the *peace* aspect of the fruit of the Spirit, and all that is encompassed n the Hebrew idea of *shalom*.

Core Values: Patience

The DNA of God #4

with Rebekah Robinson

The world has never seen a patience like that of God. For longitude and latitude, it has no rival.

This fourth volume looks at ways in which the patience of God inspires us to adopt the qualities of forbearance and grace that are so natural to Him.

www.ingramcontent.com/pod-product-compliance
Lightning Source LLC
Chambersburg PA
CBHW030034100526
44590CB00011B/198